FACING ADDICTION

Starting Recovery from Alcohol and Drugs

PATRICK CARNES, Ph.D.,

STEFANIE CARNES, Ph.D., AND JOHN BAILEY, M.D.

Gentle Path
P R E S S

Carefree, AZ

FACING ADDICTION

Starting Recovery from Alcohol and Drugs

PATRICK CARNES, Ph.D.,

STEFANIE CARNES, Ph.D., AND JOHN BAILEY, M.D.

Gentle Path
PRESS

Carefree, AZ

Gentle Path Press
PO Box 3172
Carefree, Arizona 85377
www.gentlepath.com
Copyright © 2011 by Gentle Path Press

First Edition: 2011

For more information regarding our publications,
please contact Gentle Path Press at
1-800-708-1796 (toll-free U.S. only).

Book edited by Rebecca Post
Book interior designed by Serena Castillo
Book cover by Summation Inc.

ISBN: 978-0-9826505-6-1

Contents

Acknowledgments

We would like to thank many talented people for their assistance in bringing *Facing Addiction* to fruition. It could not have happened without the support of Pine Grove Behavioral Health Center in Hattiesburg, MS and the Palm Beach Institute in West Palm Beach, FL. We are grateful to Mark Gold, M.D., Distinguished Professor and Chair of Psychiatry, University of Florida who was instrumental in bringing in John Bailey as co-author.

We are indebted to Yvonne Pearson who helped coordinate the writing of *Facing Addiction* along with Rebecca Post for her editorial guidance throughout the process. Each of us authors would like to thank individual people in our lives as well.

Stefanie Carnes would like to thank her husband Damian and her two sons Braiden and Justin, the lights of her life.

Pat Carnes would like to dedicate this book to his loving wife, Suzanne, who recently passed away. Her compassion, wisdom, love of beautiful things and youthful spirit will never be forgotten.

John Bailey would like to give thanks to his wife, April. She has provided limitless encouragement and support for the past 30 wonderful years that they have been together. She has a tremendous talent for proofreading, correcting John's numerous grammatical errors and misspellings. Without her, he vows he would probably still be delivering pizzas.

Introduction

For all addicts, a moment comes when they realize they have a problem. In this moment of lucidity, it suddenly hits home how out of control life is. Then the old rationales and cravings rush back to blur reality. Think of an addiction as being caught in a wild and dangerous whitewater stream. Those flashes of understanding enable addicts to regain stability. If they act quickly, there is a chance of escaping danger before they are pulled back into the roiling and thrilling current. Others recognize their peril and know they must get out in order to survive, but the stream is too strong and those lucid moments too rare.

There are some who have reached a point where they refuse to be pushed around any longer. They seize the opportunity and with courage and work manage to find tranquil pools or beaches. They pull themselves out and discover they had forgotten, or maybe never knew, a calmer, more ordered world. With perspective they realize the last choice they would make would be to spend their lives in the raging river. If you are looking at this book, you may be wrestling with the problem of addiction to alcohol or drugs. If you are, this doesn't mean you are bad or hopeless. It means you may have a disease from which many have healed.

If you are a normal addict, you have probably made the following statements to yourself

- Nothing will help.
- I am overreacting to normal things.
- Others (my family, my boss, my neighbors) are overreacting to normal things.
- I am worthless and too damaged to change.
- The problems will blow over.
- I can stop if I just try harder (as opposed to trying therapy or recovery).
- I will be OK if I just drink or use less.
- I will be OK if I can be more clever about my use so I will not be caught.

- The reason I do this is because of (my spouse or parents or work or religion or culture) _____ (fill in the blank).
- My situation is different.
- No one will understand what I do (or did).

If any of those thoughts occur to you, you are exactly where you should be. This is what most addicts think when first beginning to confront their addiction. If you are starting to acknowledge your problem, this is significant progress. You may be open at last to the possibility that hope and healing can enter your life. If you have reached the moment where you know that your drinking or drug use is out of control, this book is for you.

Fortunately, there are now many books on addiction (see the recommended reading list at the back of the book on page 293). However, this is the first book that takes techniques used with thousands of recovering addicts and uses these to teach you step by step how to break free from the raging current of addiction and make your life better. Decades of research and clinical experience have shown that breaking recovery into defined tasks makes it easier to leave the addictive life. As recovering people perform these tasks, they learn specific competencies with which to manage their problems. Taken together, these skills form a map for success. If they follow the map, they will reach the goal of recovery. If not, they will end up back in the whitewater.

This book is the tool many of us now in recovery wish we had when we started. It is intended to be used as part of therapy, either in an outpatient or inpatient treatment program. It is also designed to support a Twelve Step recovery program such as Alcoholics Anonymous (AA) or Narcotics Anonymous (NA). (Look for a listing of such support groups on page 266 of this book.) Please note, the content in this book is not intended to replace conference-approved materials that are published by AA or NA for use in Twelve Step meetings.

Both therapy and Twelve Step support are keys to success. Your internal addict voice will supply rationales for not doing therapy or Twelve Step work, such as:

- Therapy does not work.
- Therapists are crazy or they would not be in the business.

- Twelve Step groups will not work for me.
- I can do this on my own.
- I do not like the therapist, the group, the program, the Twelve Steps, the people there, talking about myself, or _____(fill in the blank).
- My situation is different.
- No one will understand what I do (or did).

It is at this point that addicts must try to see what is really going on because they soon will be caught up in the rapids again. That is why our first chapter explores, "What is Real?"

We have personally known many people who have died because of their addiction, and we have heard the stories of countless others who have met the same fate. Delusion is the deadliest part of this illness. Those rushing rapids kill. If you are in a moment where you can see them, we invite you to come out of the river.

Chapter One: **What Is Real?**
Recognizing Self-Delusion

Mental health is commitment to reality at all costs.
—M. Scott Peck

Addiction is an illness of escape. Its goal is to obliterate, medicate, or ignore reality. It is an alternative to letting oneself feel hurt, betrayal, worry, and—most painful of all—loneliness.

The hardest challenge for some addicts is acknowledging that they have a problem. Addiction cripples the core ability to know what is real—our most essential skill—because addicts weave a string of rationalizations and delusions that make it impossible to cope with details like jobs or families.

In this chapter, we will look at why denial holds such strong sway over addicts and what to do to counter it. We will define addiction and who is likely to become an addict.

Addiction often begins simply: reality becomes too much to bear, so we try to escape through drugs and alcohol. Escaping reality for even the briefest time brings some relief. But when escaping becomes habitual, we have a mental health illness known as addiction. If mental health can be defined, as author M. Scott Peck says, as a commitment to reality no matter what the cost, addiction can be defined as its most direct opposite: evading reality no matter the cost—though it may even bring death.

Reality distortion starts within the family. Alcoholics and drug addicts typically come from families in which addiction is already present. Often, parents, grandparents, siblings, or extended family members struggle with alcoholism, compulsive gambling, nicotine addiction, eating problems, illicit drug use, or compulsive sex. Even more likely, those family members battle a combination of addictions.

As children, addicts often grow up in an environment where there is the classic "elephant in the living room" syndrome: everyone pretends there is no problem although there's a huge issue interfering with everyone's lives. In such a situation, children learn very early to look at addiction and not see it.

People who are addicted to drugs or alcohol tend to come from families that are either rigid or chaotic. In rigid, authoritarian families all issues and problems are black and white. There is only one way to do something. They are too strict, have too much discipline, too many unbendable rules, and too many expectations for perfection. At the opposite end of the continuum are chaotic families. These families lack rules and discipline. Nothing is predictable. People's minds and expectations are constantly changing. One minute a parent may be acting like a parent and the next minute acting like a child.

In chaotic families there is not enough stability, and in rigid families there is not enough flexibility. Success in a rigid family means doing what the parents want to such an extent that children give up being who they are. In chaotic families expectations change so much that children become confused about who they are. Normal child development does not happen. By the time children enter adolescence, they have few options. Children may try to be perfect or may become rebellious. Both result in a distrust of authority and a poor sense of self. And both positions distort reality.

One essential way for people to check reality is to share with others and find out their perception of a situation. This requires a capacity for intimacy. Many addicts, however, come from families in which members are "disengaged" from one another, or at the other extreme, they are "enmeshed" with each other. In either case, children do not develop a capacity for healthy intimacy.

In disengaged families, there is little sharing, so children develop few skills about sharing, being vulnerable, or risking anything about themselves. As a result, they learn to trust no one but themselves. The further result is that self-delusion is then hard to break, and secrets become more potent than reality. The worst effect is that the children are unable to ask for help.

In enmeshed families, children learn to focus on meeting the needs of others at their own expense. Family members are very dependent on each other, and there is no sense of boundaries between themselves and others. Thus, they do not develop a strong sense of themselves. They are not capable of honest sharing because they don't have a core self to share with others. The intimacy, or closeness, they feel is a false intimacy; it is closeness built on dishonesty, even if that dishonesty is with themselves.

Addicts are also likely to have experienced trauma and abuse as children. Abuse and neglect deepen distrust of others and further distort reality. Children who are neglected conclude they are not valuable. In addition, they live with a high level of anxiety because no one teaches them common life skills or provides for their basic needs. Children find ways to deaden the anxiety they inevitably feel. They may encounter drugs at an early age and embrace those drugs when they discover that the drugs calm their anxiety. Other forms of physical and sexual abuse intensify poor self-esteem and the need for relief from fear.

Abuse victims tend to distort reality. They can overreact or under-respond to life problems. Being so terrified makes them reactive. Further, they "compartmentalize," meaning they learn to split reality, acknowledging parts of their life but disallowing or denying problem areas. That may mean acting a certain way in one context and totally different in another. They may pretend part of their life, such as a dead sibling, or a family member who is in prison, does not exist. Robert Louis Stevenson wrote about this compartmentalization when he described Dr. Jekyll and Mr. Hyde. Hyde personified the monster underneath the normal exterior of Dr. Jekyll. He was essentially describing the phenomenon of alcoholism, but it is an apt metaphor for all forms of addiction.

A final characteristic of abuse victims is that they tend to distort or minimize the impact of abuse. "It was not so bad," or, "It did not hurt me much." This adds yet another layer of reality distortion.

Addicts have so much experience in distorting reality that they become comfortable with it. Here are examples of the extremes some have gone to:

- A thirty-five-year-old pharmacist had been stealing oxycodone from the pharmacy for his own use for a year. He had been increasing the amount significantly, but he thought, because he is head of the pharmacy, he could continue to conceal his use indefinitely.
- A young man who worked as a journalist went to a crack house when he was on assignment in Jamaica. He used crack there continuously for two days, missing work. He reasoned that he was such a talented writer the magazine would not care if he missed

his deadline, so he continued to stay away from work and used crack for two more weeks.

- A sixty-year-old woman who drank to inebriation daily convinces herself she was not an alcoholic because she never drank in the morning—unless her car wouldn't start.
- A married woman traded sex for drugs, telling her husband that she was meeting girlfriends five nights a week. Even when two of her friends told her husband they had not seen her for several months, she believed she could convince her husband that the girl-friends were lying because they were mad at her.
- An executive charged hundreds of thousands of dollars to his company for televisions and computers to trade with a drug dealer for cocaine. He counted on the company's immense size and cumber-some accounting practices to bury his problem.
- A diabetic nurse continued to use increasing amounts of alcohol, convincing herself that she could monitor the amount of alcohol because she was a medical professional. This was even after going into insulin shock twice.
- A man continued to drink and drive, even after his drunken driv-ing caused a car accident that put his daughter in the hospital with a punctured lung.
- A woman drank through her second pregnancy even though her first child suffered from severe fetal alcohol syndrome and child protective services had taken the child from her.

In each of these cases, the truth came out with horrible results. Every one of these people was stunned by their capacity for self-delusion.

This is why we start by looking at denial. As you progress in recovery, you will start to understand how this process will work for you. Our purpose now is simply to say it is normal, at this point, to be confused about all this. It is also normal to punish yourself because you feel bad about your behaviors. And it is true you have not been honest with yourself or others. It will, however, be easy to see how you got to this point.

There are two challenges. First you must be honest with yourself. Then you need to be honest with those who can help you, such as your therapist or your support group.

Three activities can help you focus on reality:

1. *You must list what you think your problems are.* This list will be an important resource as you go through your recovery process.
2. *As you review these problems, notice what secrets you have.* In other words, how many instances can you find in which people are unaware of the truth. These are cases in which you have told lies, failed to tell the whole story, or decided to tell nothing at all.
3. *What excuses or rationales do you use for your addictive behavior?* Make every effort to be as honest as possible.

We will start to work here on breaking through these barriers to reality. It may be hard at first, but take heart. This process has worked for countless others before you.

Journal as a Tool

As you go through this workbook, keep a journal or notebook. You can record the "overflow" in your assignments there. Any reflections or notes you write as you go through the exercises will become invaluable to you as time goes on.

Also, find a secure place to keep your journal. If you have confidence that no one but you or a trusted confidant, such as a sponsor or therapist, will see what you have written, you can feel free to write openly. This kind of unrestricted honesty is crucial to your recovery.

Problems, Secrets, and Excuses

Problems, secrets, and excuses can block your recovery. In Worksheets 1.1–1.3 on pages 12 and 16, you will be exploring these areas of your life by creating lists under each of these categories. These worksheets are designed to discover what might be holding you back in your recovery.

The Problem List

The goal of this exercise is to reveal your current perception of what is happening in your life. It will give you a "big picture" of what brought you to this point. Making the list will assist you in talking to your therapist and others in your recovery about what is wrong.

It may feel uncomfortable or frightening at first to make this list. If necessary, take a break and come back to it later. Some addicts find that, as they write, more layers of their problems are revealed. Again, this can be unnerving, so if you need to discuss the emotions that are welling up with a sponsor or therapist, do so and then return to this exercise.

The Secret List

Usually addicts have a significant number of secrets. These are often secrets kept from spouses, partners, or family members, but may also be secrets kept from friends, neighbors, or colleagues. Addicts are experts at hiding parts of themselves. The reality for most addicts is that nobody really knows all of their secrets. These secrets might include job troubles, debt, legal problems, violent behavior, sexual acting out while intoxicated, or worries about health. In fact, many of the issues on your Problem List may exist because of the secrets they involve. You might ask yourself how many of the problems listed would be worse if everybody knew the truth about your behavior.

Secrets themselves are a problem.

First, you may carry the emotional stress of knowing you are being dishonest. Then you have the anxiety of trying to remember who you told what, so that you do not trip yourself up. And then there is the fear of discovery of the truth.

Each of these problems takes a toll on you and increases anxiety. What's worse, you end up believing some of your distortions. By telling a story often enough, an addict starts to live as if the story is the reality. You must start with reality.

Remember to include the omissions, not just the lies you have told. Your life story needs to include what you have left out.

The List of Excuses

Addicts create rationales for their behavior. Usually they state the rationale in terms of justification (I need a drink to loosen up at parties) or blame (My partner causes me to drink). Or they argue for their uniqueness; some special circumstance or situation causes them to do what they do (I have extra pressures because I'm a surgeon, priest, teacher, lawyer). Whatever the rationale, the list's purpose is to help addicts come to terms with unhealthy behavior.

It is important at the outset to label these rationales as excuses. Only when we start realizing we're making excuses can we begin stripping away the layer of lies covering our behavior.

Worksheet 1.1: **The Problem List**

Directions: List all of your problems here. Include both drug or alcohol issues (got a DWI, missed work because I had a hangover, stole to get money for drugs, and so on) and non-drug or alcohol issues (teenager having trouble in school, car transmission making funny noise).

It is important to be as complete as possible because doing so will make your recovery much stronger. If you run out of room, feel free to use another sheet of paper or write in your journal.

Problem One: _____

_____

_____

_____

Problem Two: _____

_____

_____

_____

Problem Three: _____

_____

_____

_____

Problem Four: _____

_____

_____

_____

_____

Problem Five: _____

_____

_____

_____

_____

Problem Six: _____

_____

_____

_____

_____

Problem Seven:_____

_____

_____

_____

_____

Problem Eight: _____

_____

_____

_____

_____

Problem Nine: _____

_____

_____

_____

_____

Problem Ten: _____

_____

_____

_____

_____

Problem Eleven: _____

_____

_____

_____

_____

Problem Twelve: _____

_____

_____

_____

_____

Problem Thirteen: _____

_____

_____

_____

_____

Problem Fourteen: _____

_____

_____

_____

_____

Problem Fifteen: _____

_____

_____

_____

_____

Worksheet 1.2: **The Secret List**

Directions: List each secret below and on the following pages. Also note who does not have an accurate picture about you because you have kept the secret. If you need more room, use your journal or notebook.

First Secret: _____

_____

_____

_____

_____

From whom have you kept this? _____

Second Secret: _____

_____

_____

_____

_____

From whom have you kept this? _____

Third Secret: _____

_____

_____

_____

_____

From whom have you kept this? _____

Fourth Secret: _____

_____

_____

_____

_____

From whom have you kept this? _____

Fifth Secret: _____

_____

_____

_____

_____

From whom have you kept this? _____

Sixth Secret: _____

_____

_____

_____

From whom have you kept this? _____

Seventh Secret: _____

_____

_____

_____

_____

_____

From whom have you kept this? _____

Eighth Secret: _____

_____

_____

_____

_____

From whom have you kept this? _____

Ninth Secret: _____

_____

_____

_____

_____

From whom have you kept this? _____

Tenth Secret: _____

_____

_____

_____

_____

From whom have you kept this? _____

Worksheet 1.3: **The List of Excuses**

Directions: List in the spaces below the excuses for your behavior you have used over time. Frequently, people will add to this list as they progress through the workbook. Note the date at which you realized you were distorting reality so that you can see your progress.

Rationale	Date Recognized
1.	
2.	
3.	
4.	
5.	
6.	
7.	
8.	
9.	
10.	

Rationale	Date Recognized
11.	
12.	
13.	
14.	
15.	
16.	
17.	
18.	
19.	
20.	
21.	
22.	

Rationale	Date Recognized
23.	
24.	
25.	
26.	
27.	
28.	
29.	
30.	

Consequences Inventory

Most addicts have some expectation that everyone will overlook the damage caused by what they do. Some become indignant when they do experience consequences—getting demoted or fired, bouncing checks, or going to jail.

Consequences, however, are signposts to reality. Addicts receive them because the world does not share their thought distortion. Lies, broken promises, and exploitive behavior will eventually cost, and cost dearly.

In these ways, addicts discover that their denial is the beginning of a grief process. In other words, the losses begin mounting and the addict tries to stave off the moment of truth by clinging to denial. Ultimately, that moment arrives and disaster is at hand.

Addicts find it extremely useful to do a complete inventory of their consequences. All addicts who have experienced out-of-control behavior, used getting drunk or high to cope with stress, or stolen money to buy drugs, have had consequences due to their behavior. You have had consequences, too.

Sadly, people sometimes don't call what has happened to them "consequences," or they use drugs or alcohol as a way to avoid having to feel or to admit what has happened. Though it is difficult to face the "wreckage of our past," as Alcoholics Anonymous puts it, an honest assessment of your consequences will dramatically improve your recovery.

Worksheet 1.4: **Consequences Inventory**

Directions: Look realistically at the consequences of your behavior in each of the categories below. Put a check in the box by each of the ones that you have experienced.

Emotional Consequences

- ❑ 1. Thoughts or feelings about committing suicide
- ❑ 2. Attempted suicide
- ❑ 3. Homicidal thoughts or feelings
- ❑ 4. Feelings of hopelessness and despair
- ❑ 5. Failed efforts to control your behavior
- ❑ 6. Feeling like you had two different lives—one public and one secret
- ❑ 7. Depression, paranoia, or fear of going insane
- ❑ 8. Loss of touch with reality
- ❑ 9. Loss of self-esteem
- ❑ 10. Loss of life goals
- ❑ 11. Acting against your own values and beliefs
- ❑ 12. Strong feelings of guilt and shame
- ❑ 13. Strong feelings of isolation and loneliness
- ❑ 14. Strong fears about the future
- ❑ 15. Emotional exhaustion
- ❑ 16. Other emotional consequences: _____

_____

Physical Consequences

- ❑ 1. Continuation of addictive behavior, despite the risk to health
- ❑ 2. Extreme weight loss or gain
- ❑ 3. Physical problems (ulcers, high blood pressure, etc.)
- ❑ 4. Physical injury or abuse by others
- ❑ 5. Involvement in potentially abusive or dangerous situations
- ❑ 6. Vehicle accidents (automobile, motorcycle, bicycle)
- ❑ 7. Injury to yourself from your drinking or drugging behavior
- ❑ 8. Sleep disturbances (not enough sleep, too much sleep)

□   9. Physical exhaustion

□ 10. Other physical consequences related to your drinking or using drugs, such as kidney problems, dental problems, or hepatitis:

_____

Spiritual Consequences

□ 1. Feelings of spiritual emptiness

□ 2. Feeling disconnected from yourself and the world

□ 3. Feeling abandoned by God or your Higher Power

□ 4. Anger at your Higher Power or God

□ 5. Loss of faith in anything spiritual

□ 6. Other spiritual consequences:_____

_____

Consequences Related to Family

□ 1. Risking the loss of partner or spouse

□ 2. Loss of partner or spouse

□ 3. Increase in marital or relationship problems

□ 4. Jeopardizing the well-being of your family

□ 5. Loss of family's or partner's respect

□ 6. Increase in problems with your children

□ 7. Estrangement from your family of origin

□ 8. Other family or partnership consequences: _____

_____

Career and Educational Consequences

□ 1. Decrease in work productivity

□ 2. Demotion at work

□ 3. Loss of coworkers' respect

□ 4. Loss of the opportunity to work in the career of your choice

□ 5. Failing grades in school

□ 6. Loss of educational opportunities

□ 7. Loss of business

❑   8. Forced to change careers
❑   9. Not working to your level of capability
❑ 10. Termination of job
❑ 11. Other career or educational consequences:_____

_____

Other Consequences

❑   1. Loss of important friendships
❑   2. Loss of interest in hobbies or activities
❑   3. Few or no friends who don't drink or take drugs
❑   4. Financial problems
❑   5. Illegal activities (arrests or near-arrests)
❑   6. Court or legal involvement
❑   7. Lawsuits
❑   8. Prison or workhouse
❑   9. Stealing or embezzling to support behavior
❑ 10. Other consequences:_____

_____

You will need to refer to this inventory later in this book. In addition, it would be of great benefit to you to talk about it with your therapist or sponsor for later work.

This is the tough part. Often addicts will feel that consequences are unfair. Remember that no one promised you justice and fairness. You have to deal with what is real. You may have lived with the illusion that others will respond to perceived inequities or will be sympathetic because of all the good you have done or how hard you have tried. None of that will help you now.

The people who gave you the consequences are not your enemies. By seeing those who give the consequences as the enemy, you keep yourself stuck in justifying your behavior. The real problem is your denial and your capacity for self-delusion. You are responsible for making yourself vulnerable to them. When you chose your behavior, you opened the door to consequences. You have to ask whether the risk was worth it. And if you can do this, you've already made significant progress toward recovery.

What helps at this point is to see your consequences as your teachers. You have been sent a lesson to learn. If you don't learn the lesson this time, it will manifest itself again, and probably in a more painful form next time. A poet named Portia Nelson expressed it this way:

Autobiography in Five Short Chapters

By Portia Nelson

I

I walk down the street.
There is a deep hole in the sidewalk
I fall in.
I am lost…I am helpless.
It isn't my fault.
It takes me forever to find a way out.

II

I walk down the same street.
There is a deep hole in the sidewalk.
I pretend I don't see it.
I fall in again.
I can't believe I am in the same place

But, it isn't my fault.
It still takes a long time to get out.

III
I walk down the same street.
There is a deep hole in the sidewalk.
I see it is there.
I still fall in…it's a habit.
My eyes are open
I know where I am.
It is my fault.
I get out immediately.

IV
I walk down the same street.
There is a deep hole in the sidewalk.
I walk around it.

V
I walk down another street.

Denial

To deny something is to say it is not true, to say "no" to it, or to prevent it from happening. Denial, of course, can be an honest, straightforward disagreement or refusal. When coupled with out-of-control drinking or drugging behavior, however, denial becomes a potent, powerful, and often destructive way of protecting oneself from reality—and from help.

For addicts, denial is a confused kind of thinking and reasoning used to avoid the reality of behavior or the consequences of behavior. It is a way to try to manage and explain the chaos caused by addictive behavior. It is an effort to protect drinking and drug use that addicts believe they can't live without. It is a way to deflect attention and responsibility. Here are some examples:

- It isn't like I'm using every night.
- My kids aren't hurt because I only use when they're sleeping or not at home.
- I work hard; I have to have a way to relax.
- A lot of people use marijuana.
- I am an adult and can make my own decisions.
- It doesn't affect my job.
- If you think I'm bad, you should see so-and-so.
- My situation is different.

Worksheet 1.5: **Denial**

Directions: This exercise will help you look at the role denial is playing in your life. List all of the reasons you believed—or still believe—you don't belong in therapy or a group for your drinking or drug use.

1. _____

2. _____

3. _____

4. _____

5. _____

6. _____

7. _____

8. _____

9. _____

10. _____

11. _____

12. _____

13. _____

14. _____

15. _____

16. _____

17. _____

18. _____

19. _____

20. _____

There are many kinds of denial. A few of the primary categories follow. Write your own examples of each type in the space provided.

Global Thinking. Attempting to justify why something is not a problem using terms like "always," "never," "no problem whatsoever."

_____

_____

_____

_____

_____

_____

_____

Rationalization. Justifying unacceptable behavior. "I don't have a problem—I just like a drink once in awhile." "Everyone I know uses a little cocaine on the weekend."

_____

_____

_____

_____

_____

_____

_____

Minimizing. Trying to make behavior or consequences seem smaller and less important than they are. "Only a little." "Only once in awhile." "It is no big deal."

_____

_____

_____

_____

_____

_____

_____

Comparison. Shifting the focus to someone else to justify behaviors. "I'm not as bad as _____."

_____

_____

_____

_____

_____

_____

_____

Uniqueness. Thinking you are different or special. "My situation is different." "I was hurt more." "That's fine for you, but I'm too busy to go to group right now."

_____

_____

_____

_____

_____

_____

Avoiding by creating an uproar or distraction. Being a clown and getting everyone laughing; angry outbursts meant to frighten; threats and posturing; shocking behavior; focusing on a relationship.

_____

_____

_____

_____

_____

_____

Avoiding by omission. Trying to change the subject, ignore the subject, or manipulate the conversation to avoid talking about something. It is also leaving out important bits of information, like the fact that you couldn't find where you parked the car in the morning because you had a blackout when you drove home the night before.

_____

_____

_____

_____

_____

_____

_____

Blaming. "Well, you would drink at night, too, if you had my job." "If my wife/husband/partner weren't so cold, I wouldn't have to go to the bar at night." "I can't help it. The baby cries day and night and makes me nervous, so I need something to relax."

_____

_____

_____

_____

_____

_____

_____

Intellectualizing. Avoiding feelings and responsibility by thinking or by asking why. Explaining everything. Getting lost in detail and storytelling. Pretending superior intellect and using intelligence as a weapon.

_____

_____

_____

_____

_____

_____

_____

Hopelessness/helplessness. "I'm a victim, I can't help it." "There is nothing I can do to get better." "I'm the worst."

_____

_____

_____

_____

_____

_____

_____

Manipulative behavior. Usually involves some distortion of reality including the use of power, lies, secrets, or guilt to exploit others. "What they don't know won't hurt them." "I'll get better if you do x, y, or z."

_____

_____

_____

_____

_____

_____

_____

Compartmentalizing. Separating your life into compartments in which you do things that you keep separate from other parts of your life.

_____

_____

_____

_____

_____

_____

_____

Crazy-making. When confronted by others who do have a correct perception, telling them they are totally wrong. Acting indignantly toward them is an attempt to make them feel crazy by telling them, in a sense, that they cannot trust their own perceptions.

_____

_____

_____

_____

_____

_____

_____

Seduction. The use of charm, humor, good looks, or helpfulness for personal gain and to cover up insincerity.

_____

_____

_____

_____

_____

_____

_____

There Really is No Excuse

Most addicts discover there really is no excuse for their behavior. It is not easy to be honest with oneself, much less to be honest with the rest of the world. But staying in denial and staying dishonest guarantees staying in old, destructive patterns of behavior.

Accountability

When you begin to accept responsibility for your behaviors and their consequences, you will get a glimmer of what life in recovery can be. You know all too well that denial creates constant anxiety. The good news is that honesty and accountability bring peace and freedom, a feeling of serenity that comes from integrity.

In denial, you say that you did not hurt anyone; accountability is facing the fact that you hurt others. For example, if you get high and isolate yourself, you might not recognize any damage to others. Yet if you are unavailable to your partner or so preoccupied that the kids are neglected, the impact and the damage are very real.

Powerless or Pointless

In addiction recovery, we talk about powerlessness. Because of your addiction, you have been unable to stop your behavior on your own. That is why you have asked for help. Despite the fact that you are powerless, you are still responsible and accountable for what you have done. The concept of accountability is central to the Twelve Step process. Accepting accountability helps you to break through denial and admit the extent of the problem.

Worksheet 1.6: **Powerless or Pointless**

Directions: In the space that follows, list as many examples as possible of people who were hurt by your behavior and in what ways they were hurt. Make your examples as concrete as possible. This task is one of the hardest in recovery. Though it will be painful, it is not about punishing yourself; it is about facing reality and leaving denial behind. So be gentle with yourself, but also be thorough.

1. _____
   _____
   _____
   _____
   _____

2. _____
   _____
   _____
   _____
   _____

3. _____
   _____
   _____
   _____
   _____

Facing Addiction: Starting Recovery from Alcohol and Drugs

4. _____

_____

_____

_____

_____

5. _____

_____

_____

_____

_____

6. _____

_____

_____

_____

_____

7. _____

_____

_____

_____

_____

8. _____

   _____

   _____

   _____

   _____

9. _____

   _____

   _____

   _____

   _____

10. _____

   _____

   _____

   _____

   _____

If you are like most addicts, you are starting to realize how far from reality you have been living. To reassure yourself that you are not alone, we have included comments from other addicts describing what this phase was like for them. As you read, note how reality inserted itself in their lives:

- Used a dirty needle and got hepatitis.
- Stole a hundred dollars from my brother to buy drugs.
- Left kids alone when I went to buy drugs.
- Spent grocery money on cocaine and kids went hungry at end of month.
- Hit my wife when I was drunk.
- Exchanged sex for drugs.
- Embarrassed my daughter when I got drunk and passed out at her wedding.
- Kept using meth even when it was ruining my teeth.
- Missed important work meeting because of a hangover.
- Lost my best friend because I slept with her boyfriend.
- Ended up in a bar when I promised myself I wouldn't.
- Lost two jobs because I missed so many days of work.
- Lost my drivers license due to DWIs.
- Accumulated heavy debt to buy heroine.
- Got arrested for bar fight.
- Kept using drugs despite my promises not to and my wife left.
- Got mugged when I was high.
- Kept drinking with my boyfriend even though he beat me when he got drunk.
- I was thirty years old and tried to pick up a high school girl when I was high.
- Flunked out of college when I smoked so much marijuana I couldn't study.
- Let my kids hang out at a meth cooking site with me.
- Kept using crack when kids were home despite involvement of child protection.
- Put myself in a dangerous situation with strangers.
- Missed my son's high school graduation ceremony because I was high.

- Woke up in bed with two strangers.
- Had all my credit cards and cash stolen when I was high.
- Hit a pedestrian when I was driving drunk.
- Hawked my grandmother's wedding ring to get money for oxycodone.
- Had a child born with Fetal Alcohol Syndrome.
- When I was fourteen, got caught stealing car stereos.
- Got fired for embezzlement.
- The police found me passed out on the couch, my baby crying beside me.
- Ran up $5,000 on my employer's credit card buying stuff to exchange for crack.
- Threw a plate at my husband when I was intoxicated.

You are not alone. These are people who managed to change their lives dramatically. They started by admitting they needed help.

Getting the Help You Need

After realizing that you have a problem—even though you may not want to call it an addiction—there are two necessary steps.

1. You must start therapy.
2. You must join a Twelve Step program for drug or alcohol addiction.

It is quite common at this stage to wonder if you are really an addict and need to go through all this. The next two chapters will help you decide whether you are or not.

It's also important to understand that, if addiction is a problem in your life, this book will not help you recover if you use it in isolation. Because of the shame and guilt addiction involves, it's tempting to think, "I'll just pick up the materials, do them at home, and talk to you when I'm all better." You must talk with people who have more experience in recovery than you. It is the nature of denial to reassert itself when a person becomes isolated from others. Your ability to recognize your addiction and its consequences in your life and in the lives of others increases dramatically when you are with people who have struggled as you have. "Stick with the winners," urges Alcoholics Anonymous, meaning find people who have walked in the same shadows now clouding your life, and who are now standing in the light.

Therapists are trained to help people understand what is happening to them—you can get an important perspective from them. What's more, therapists are trained to guide you over time and can help you through what can be a painful and bewildering process.

If you already have a therapist, he or she may have handed you this book. Your therapist will become one of your guides for this process. Our experience in working with addicts has taught us about what an addict has to do to heal and find sustained recovery—and that is what this book offers you. We know, too, that it doesn't happen overnight—the process takes three to five years.

Be aware that our research has shown that Twelve Step work and therapy are linked in an essential way. While therapy accelerates the process and dramatically reduces the risk of relapse, therapy alone is not enough. The Twelve Step process is indispensable for recovery. Being in a community of supportive people who are also recovering addicts is absolutely key to recovery.

There are several ways you can find recovery groups. Start by looking in the Resources list at the back of this book. Your therapist may also be able to connect you with a person who can serve as a temporary sponsor. Your local medical or psychological information and referral services may be of help. Also, look in the phone book. For a guide to fellowships at a national level that can put you in touch with someone in your community, check website listings at the back of the book. Once you find a group, it takes a lot of courage to walk through those doors. But this is a path to the kind of healing and wholeness you've looked for all your life.

Finding a Sponsor

One of the great traditions that has grown out of the Twelve Step movement is sponsorship. A sponsor is another individual with more recovery experience whom we ask to help us work through our own recovery and healing. We seek out someone who has what we want—serenity, wisdom, humor—or who has walked a similar path. It's perfectly all right to find a temporary sponsor, someone who can help you understand the Twelve Step process and language when you're beginning recovery.

You may feel awkward asking someone to be your sponsor, especially when you are new in the program. You may assume you are imposing on them, and this may hold you back from reaching out for help. Overcoming these negative assumptions becomes a way of nurturing yourself, and it is a crucial first step in the road to recovery. Start by sharing all that you know with your therapist and with your sponsor. Use the exercises in this chapter to help you talk with them.

By reading this chapter, you've taken a significant step. Breaking free from denial is one of the hardest steps we addicts take. If you need to take a break or nurture yourself in some way (eating in a nice restaurant, enjoying a hot bath, going for a walk on a beautiful evening), give that to yourself. And know that the strength you need to continue will be given to you.

Chapter Two: **What Is an Addictive System?**
Understanding Addictive Behavior

…every addict engages in a relationship with an object or event in order to produce a desired mood change, state of intoxication, or trance state.
—from The Addictive Personality, *by Craig Nakken*

We have come a long way in understanding addiction, but progress has not been easy. There was a period in the 1930s and the 1940s when alcoholics and drug addicts were seen as untreatable. Compulsive gamblers were, at best, objects of curiosity and more often deemed people without character. Sexual acting out and binge eating were perceived to be moral problems, if they were talked about at all.

Today we understand that addiction is an illness, a very serious disease. Furthermore, problems such as drug, food, gambling, and sex addiction are actually related and rely on similar physical processes. Most important, we know that people can get help and that a good prognosis exists.

One definition used to describe addiction is that it is a pathological relationship with a mood-altering experience that the person continues to engage in despite adverse consequences. People who grow up in difficult family situations learn not to trust. As adults, they search for something to trust and rely on to relieve the pervasive unease they feel. Since alcohol and drugs always do what they promise, at least temporarily, they often become the answer, thus the pathological relationship begins.

For alcoholics and drug addicts, the bottle or the drug becomes the priority for which they sacrifice everything. They put alcohol and drugs before their children, spouses, and friends, despite great cost to themselves. They have an affair with the bottle or the powder or the pipe.

Addiction has a physiological component. In the mid-1970s, scientists started to understand that addiction reflected a problem in the brain. Certain behaviors or drugs stimulate the brain to release "pleasure chemicals." People escape difficult feelings by repeatedly using the behaviors or drugs that release the pleasure chemicals. Eventually this continuous stimulation actually changes the way the brain works. People lose control and the behaviors become compulsive. Compulsion is at the core of the addictive process.

It is important that you understand how the pleasure chemical is triggered, how the behavior becomes compulsive, and how your brain is changed by addiction. You will learn more about this in the next chapter.

Recognizing Addiction

When a person has developed an addiction, you will usually see certain destructive behaviors. These are:

- **Compulsive use.** If the alcohol or drug is available, the addict uses too much of it, and uses it often.
- **Impaired control.** When an addict tries to use, control is lost and usually a single use is followed by many more. As is often heard in Narcotics Anonymous, "one use is too many and a thousand is not enough."
- **Continued use despite harm or consequences.** Addicts keep using alcohol or drugs even when it causes health, relationship, job, or legal problems.
- **Craving.** The desire for alcohol or a drug can change in intensity from minute to minute. It can even seem to disappear during abstinent periods. But using even a tiny amount can wake up cravings and trigger continued use. People, places, and things associated with use in the past can also wake up cravings.
- **Denial.** There is a saying that "addiction is the only disease that tells you that you don't have it." The degree that an addict can minimize drug use or consequences is one of the most striking and common manifestations of addiction, as well as one of the most baffling to others. Breaking through this denial is an important component of addiction treatment.

Am I an Addict?

People who are using too much often wonder whether they are really addicted. They wonder if they are having a problem with substance abuse or substance dependence. It is possible that you may be having both problems. The main difference between the two is that increased tolerance and withdrawal symptoms are part of the diagnosis for dependency. Typically an individual starts abusing drugs and alcohol, then the use progresses to dependency.

Worksheet 2.1: **Abuse or Dependence?**

Directions: Fill out this worksheet to help you understand whether you are having a problem with abuse or dependence. Please check all that apply to you.

Abuse:

_____ I continue to use even though I can't keep my obligations at work, school, or home.

_____ I continue to use even in potentially hazardous situations, such as driving.

_____ I continue to use even though I have had legal problems because of my use.

_____ I continue to use even when my use has caused problems in my relationships.

Dependence:

_____ I need more alcohol or drugs to get high (Increased tolerance).

_____ If I don't use, I get irritable, have a racing heart, feel shaky, or have other uncomfortable physical sensations.

_____ I find myself using more than I mean to.

_____ I can't seem to stop using even though I want to.

_____ I spend too much of my time using, or feeling sick after I've used.

_____ I continue to use even though it interferes with my normal daily activities, including work, school, household chores, and relationships.

_____ I continue to use despite negative consequences.

If you checked one item under abuse or three under dependence, you probably are demonstrating signs of abuse or dependency. The symptoms that professionals look for in diagnosing abuse or dependence are the same as the ones in the checklist you just completed. Though it can be frightening to realize you have a serious problem, many addicts find it helpful and relieving to recognize and admit it. Remember, this is the beginning of a healing process that will work for you.

The Addictive System

Jim didn't always use alcohol compulsively. When he was in college he would get drunk once in awhile. When he had finished finals and had a week ahead with no classes, he figured he deserved to let go. That's when he would party with his friends and get completely wasted. But he was careful not to get drunk when he was in the middle of a term. Hangovers just did not go well with studying. Besides, his dad was an alcoholic. Jim hated his dad's behavior when he was drinking, and he didn't want to be like him.

After college Jim got a job as a stockbroker. By the time he was thirty he was married and had a young child. He was working sixty hours a week and then would come home to his wife complaining that he was always gone. On weekends he was inundated with house chores and helping with his son. It felt like a never-ending merry-go-round of stress to him, and he found a drink helped him relax. He would walk in the house, the stress would mount, and he would go to the cabinet and mix himself a martini. Within a short time he'd feel that sweet feeling of mellowness spreading through his body.

After awhile, though, it took two martinis, and then three, before he'd feel that sweet feeling. On Sunday mornings he would look forward to a little time to read the paper and drink his coffee, but when their second child was born, the time for that seemed to disappear. By noon he would feel so stressed that he would open a bottle of wine with lunch. He knew it wasn't a good idea because he would end up getting tired and distracted and not accomplish what he needed to. But he couldn't stop himself. Just the thought of the cork popping, the thought of how the wine would sound pouring into the glass, would make his muscles begin to relax.

By the time Jim was thirty-five years old, he was waiting for noon to come every day when he could justify popping the cork. His body was craving the fluid that would take his stress away. The martini at night had turned into several, one right after the other, just to make him feel like he could function. His wife would nag him about not drinking so much, so he would stop at a bar just to have one drink before he got home. This would turn into two or three drinks. He did this even on the nights when he took his son to Boy Scouts or other activities. He didn't plan to have more than one drink on those nights, but he would find himself ordering a second and third even while telling himself that he shouldn't. He would later rationalize that he could drive his son anyway because he could hold his liquor. Jim had become an addict.

Kathy's addiction developed more quickly. She grew up in a home where her mother and father fought most of the time. Her father occasionally hit her mother, and Kathy was afraid to leave the house for too long a time. She was worried about what might happen to her mother when she was gone. She continued to live at home when she began community college, but it was exciting to meet a new group of friends. She was out one evening with her new friends when one of them pulled out a pipe. Kathy said she had to get home. She didn't tell her friends, but she was worrying about her mother. Her father had been laid off at work recently and his temper was running high. One of her friends noticed that she seemed jumpy. He encouraged her to just take one puff of the crack cocaine, said it would help her mellow out. She said, "OK, just one."

Just one hit made her feel so much better. She soon began to rely on crack to help her stop worrying about her mother and father and allow herself to hang out with her friends instead. She would go to her room when she got home from school and lay out her homework. Then she would put on the music she listened to with her new friends. The music put her in the mood, and pretty soon she would close her books and reach for her pipe. Her grades began to slip, and she decided she was going to stop. But as soon as somebody pulled out the pipe again, she held out her hand. She would think to herself, "I shouldn't do this," but it didn't matter. Her hand was reaching for the pipe anyway.

Addiction is a self-reinforcing system. Once you have become addicted, you are caught in a spin cycle that is hard to escape. Understanding addiction as a repetitive system will help you identify what in your life needs to change.

The addiction cycle is embedded in a larger addictive system which starts with a belief system. The belief system is a collection of convictions, myths, and values that affect the decisions we make. Beliefs about families, careers, relationships, and ourselves are usually part of this internal paradigm.

At the core of this belief system are ideas you hold to be true about yourself. For addicts, these beliefs are often riddled with toxic shame—a profound sense of worthlessness or inadequacy. The delusional thinking we explored in the first chapter flows out of these core beliefs, rooted in toxic shame. This impaired thinking allows the addictive cycle to flourish. It essentially distorts reality or even blocks your awareness of what is going on around you. These rationalizations and justifications allow the addict to ignore key realities such as a deadline at work or financial limits.

The Addictive Cycle

Kathy and Jim are caught in the addictive cycle. The cycle starts off with preoccupation, which involves obsession about alcohol or drugs, about when and how to get the drugs. Jim would plan how he was going to get enough alcohol to feel okay during the evening without his wife knowing how much he was drinking. He obsessed about leaving work early enough to stop at the bar on his way home. Many days Kathy couldn't listen in class because she was preoccupied with figuring out how she was going to get some more crack.

These obsessions are intensified through the use of ritual. Jim would regularly stop at the bar on his way home from work, telling himself he'd only have one. Kathy would listen to the music she associated with crack. The atmosphere of the bar, the atmosphere created by the music, put distance between reality and obsession with the alcohol or drugs.

The next phase of the cycle is the compulsive use. The tensions addicts feel are reduced by using. They feel better for awhile, thanks to the pleasure chemicals triggered in their brains. Jim drank every day, whether it interfered with his life or not. Kathy used crack cocaine on a daily basis, even when her grades were crashing. They used compulsively. It felt to them like they no longer had a choice.

Very soon reality sets in. Often addicts will see the significance of their behavior and feel ashamed. Jim felt awash in shame when he walked into the house and saw his son waiting for him in his Boy Scout uniform, an hour late for their meeting. Addicts often face more severe consequences than this. Consider the man who became too drunk to notice when his young son was drowning in a pool. His shame and regret consumed him, driving his addiction to escalate further until he lost his whole family. The same was true for the woman who killed someone when she was driving under the influence. Or think about the man whose arm had to be amputated when the needle track marks got infected. He felt horrible when he fully realized that his choices had resulted in the disfigurement.

This point of the cycle is a painful place that addicts generally visit many times. Each time they are at this low point, they probably promise themselves they will never do it again. Yet once again, they use, and that leads to despair. For many addicts, this dark emotion brings on depression or a chronic feeling of hopelessness. One easy way to cure feelings of despair is to start obsessing again. The cycle then perpetuates itself and life becomes unmanageable.

In summary, the addictive cycle becomes the driving force in the addict's life. It starts with a core belief in your worthlessness. Here are some examples of core beliefs:

- I am not good enough.
- I am stupid, ugly, and worthless.
- No one will ever really love me.
- I am never going to be successful.

Your thinking becomes impaired. Here are some examples of impaired thinking:

- I am not hurting anybody with my behavior.
- I deserve to have a drink or use this drug.
- I don't have much to live for, so I might as well get drunk.

You become preoccupied with drugs or alcohol. Here are some examples of preoccupation:

- I use a different liquor store for each day of the week, so people won't know how much I am drinking.
- I plan several months ahead of time how to get enough alcohol for vacation and where to hide it.

You start using rituals to put some distance between yourself and your behavior. Here are some examples of ritualizations:

- I always wear the same pair of boots when I am going out to hit the town.
- I always make martinis at five o'clock when I get home from work.
- I put on the same music before I smoke.

As you use more, your use becomes compulsive. Here are some examples of compulsive behavior:

- I must have at least two drinks to start my day.
- If I am feeling stressed, I automatically reach for a pain killer.
- When I am going to a party I cannot go in without having several hits of weed.

Bad things start to happen. Consequences start to occur. You find yourself despairing about how complex, stressful, or awful your life has become. Here are some examples of despair:

- I wake up the day after I've tied one on and feel suicidal.
- I worry about who I am going to disappoint and feel shame and guilt.
- I don't go to work, because I can't face my boss.

Life has become unmanageable. Because you are out of control—and also out of touch with reality—the problems compound. Lies, covering up, and inventing ways to keep the losses at bay do not stop the accumulation. Sooner or later, your life becomes a mess.

Here are some examples of unmanageability:

- I lost our family business.
- I was rejected by roommates several times because of drug-using behavior.
- I became suicidal because of my years of ecstasy use.

As your life becomes more and more unmanageable, the feelings of despair confirm your dysfunctional beliefs about being an unlovable person. You used alcohol and drugs to escape the feelings of anxiety, depression, and hopelessness, but now the system perpetuates itself.

Diagram Your Own Addictive System

Some people have found it helpful to map out their own addictive system. Figure 2.1 on page 55 is a graphic map of how the system looks. Take each component—beliefs, thinking, addiction cycle, and unmanageability—and map out what happens in your addiction. In each blank space on page 55, write examples that apply to your life. Provide as many examples as you can.

The Addictive System

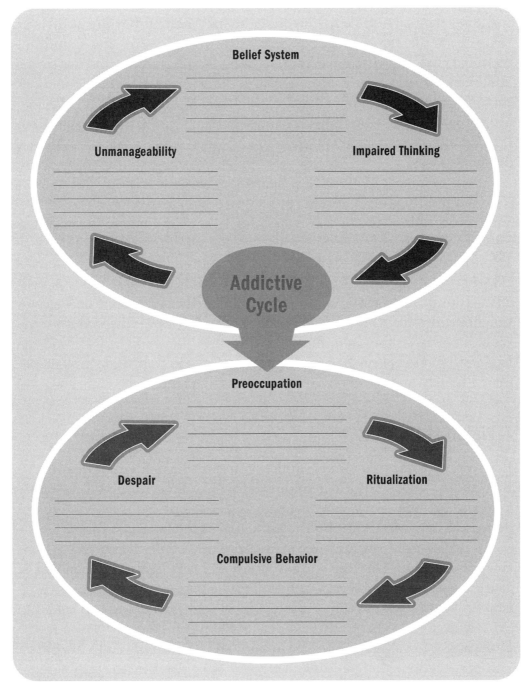

Figure 2.1

Starting Recovery

Starting recovery can seem bleak at first. Addicts typically are mired in the crises they face while they wonder about whether they are addicts or not. Add to this the almost certain fact that they are receiving significant consequences and reactions from spouses, family members, employers, and even their therapists. Another worry is the growing realization that this addiction is bigger than they ever realized. Many addicts feel like they are not ready to take on drastic changes in their lives. Others may feel relief about recovery but worry about their losses. All feel that their life has become a mess.

In moments like this it is helpful to remember the experience of Vice Admiral James Stockdale, who was a prisoner of war during the Vietnam conflict. He has the record for being the longest incarcerated POW of the war and is highly regarded for the number of men he was able to keep alive to survive the camps and the war. Years later he was asked how he survived such a hopeless situation. His response was very clear. He said that, each day, he had to think that he would be successful. He had to have absolute faith that not only would he get out but he would thrive. At the same time that he held this vision in his mind, he had to be aware of how bad things were today. Survival depended on being ruthlessly honest about the challenges of the moment.

A Vision of the Future

Recovering from addiction is similar: you must have a vision of your future and an absolutely clear understanding of how miserable your life has become. Before we focus on the challenges of the moment, we are going to ask you to think about your vision of the future.

Let us fast forward three years from now. Imagine you have been successful in your sobriety and put your life back together in new ways. Use the space and questions on the following pages to think through a vision of what recovery might be like. Think about what you feel called to do. Perhaps it is to help other addicts in recovery. Perhaps it is to teach. Perhaps it is to cultivate your spirituality and help others cultivate theirs. Perhaps it is something entirely different. Take the time to supply detail to your vision by being specific about how your life would be different.

For the moment suspend all your current problems and lay out the vision of your recovery future as you most earnestly desire it. This may feel artificial and unreal at first. You may doubt your ability to change or doubt you deserve good things. It may be hard to take your attention from the current problems, but laying out your vision will help you clarify many issues and provide perspective. Remember, this vision will evolve as your recovery progresses.

Worksheet 2.2: **Your Long-Term Goals**

Directions: Be specific in the vision that you want. Take the time and use the space provided to create a viable image of successful recovery for yourself in a three-year time frame:

Your family life

What changes would occur among your relationships? Be specific about who and what would be different.

_____

_____

_____

_____

_____

_____

Your work life

What would be the focus of your career energy? How would you work differently? Is there a significant career shift in your future? What are the most rewarding things you can do?

_____

_____

_____

_____

_____

_____

Your social life

Recovery often means a significant change in friends and peers. It can also mean that activities change. Sometimes it means overcoming isolation. What changes do you foresee?

_____

_____

_____

_____

_____

_____

Your time

Most likely, much of your time went into your addiction. Yet time is really all we have. How do you picture spending your time in the future?

_____

_____

_____

_____

_____

_____

Your rewards

You used your addiction because of its huge rewards, despite its great cost. How will you replace these rewards? What will make you feel good, relax you, or energize you? What will be a priority now?

_____

_____

_____

_____

_____

_____

Your physical well being

Consider what your body will be like. Many addicts have not taken care of themselves well. What physical changes would you make? Other changes will be important to you. Every addict has unique circumstances. What specific changes for you and your family do you see as important that we have not listed? Are there things you have always wanted to do but have never done? What would those be?

_____

_____

_____

_____

_____

_____

From Addictive System to Recovery System

Now that you have a clear vision in mind, it is important to be equally clear about your present reality. Addiction keeps you from seeing reality, and not seeing reality keeps you addicted. On page 55, you diagrammed your addictive system. Remember these components of the addictive system:

- You hold core beliefs that you are unworthy and that your needs will go unmet.
- Your thinking has become distorted in some significant ways through denial, delusion, and minimization.
- The addiction cycle starts with preoccupation and soon becomes obsession.
- Rituals are established around drug or alcohol use, such as going to the same bar and listening to certain types of music.
- You develop compulsive behaviors.
- Despair follows and you are mired in shame and guilt.
- Your life becomes unmanageable.

You do not have to remain caught in this cycle. The addictive system—a system that destroys us—can be transformed into a recovery system that renews us. The components of the addictive system are transformed into:

- core beliefs in which you accept that you are worthy of love and having your needs met
- thinking that is empowering, honest, and clear
- a focus on things that matter most with little attention given to things that are unimportant
- new rituals that deepen awareness and help to access your own wisdom
- "zone behaviors" in which you focus on being at your very best and are committed to something "bigger than yourself"
- happiness, success, and affirmation, because you are doing what you are best at and what means the most to you

The outcome of the renewal cycle is resilience. You have margin and reserves when challenges occur. Grief, hurt, and disappointment deepen your resolve and add depth to who you are. When you filled out your vision of the future, you were articulating what your life will be like in the recovery system.

Diagram Your Own Recovery System

Some people have found it helpful to map out their own recovery system. Figure 2.2 on page 63 is a graphic map of how the system looks. Take each component—beliefs, resilience, empowered thinking, renewal cycle, focus, rewards, rituals and the resulting zone behavior—and map out what you expect to happen in your recovery. In each blank space, write examples that apply to your life. Provide as many examples as you can.

Obstacles to Recovery

You will now identify the obstacles you must overcome and the specific steps you must take to overcome them so you can transform your addictive system to a recovery system. Your challenge is to determine what it will take to transform your life from being dominated by an addictive system to being empowered by recovery. Worksheet 2.3 on page 64 is extremely helpful early in recovery to give you perspective on the groundwork necessary to sustain the changes you must make.

The Recovery System

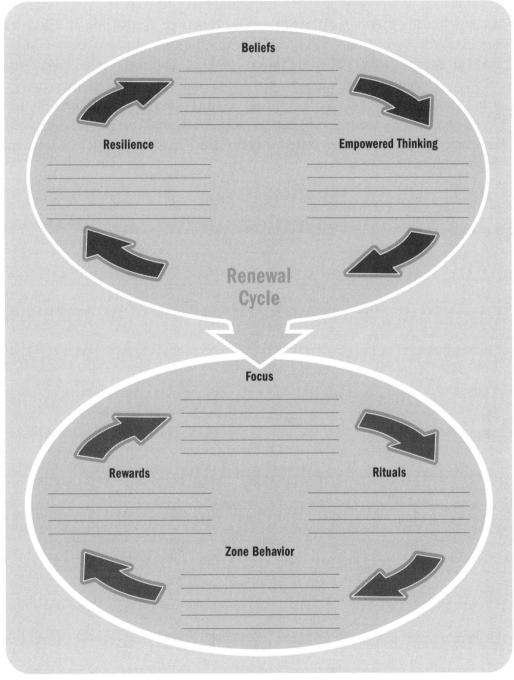

Figure 2.2

Worksheet 2.3: **Obstacles to Recovery**

Directions: List the major obstacles that you will need to overcome to achieve your recovery goals. Obstacles might include having to set boundaries with using friends, having to cope with pain or depression, not knowing what you want to do with your life, fighting with your spouse all the time, or dealing with a chronic illness such as diabetes. Name the difficulties and describe in detail why they are challenging. Remember, being honest with yourself is critical, in order to see your situation as it really is. Do not hold on to false hopes, denial, and delusional thinking. After you have selected 10 obstacles, transfer them onto The Systems Transformer (Figure 2.3) on page 68.

1. _____

   _____

   _____

2. _____

   _____

   _____

3. _____

   _____

   _____

4. _____

   _____

   _____

5. _____

_____

_____

6. _____

_____

_____

7. _____

_____

_____

8. _____

_____

_____

9. _____

_____

_____

10. _____

_____

_____

Worksheet 2.4: **Steps to Take Toward Recovery**

Directions: Make your best effort to specify steps that, if taken, would bring you closer to a true recovery system and reverse the polarity and energy of the old addictive one. Identify action steps that correspond with the obstacles you chose in Worksheet 2.3 on page 64. The steps will mean change and that may mean significant loss. But if the task is well done, you will have laid out the basics of a plan for the next two to five years of recovery. By sharing this with peers, sponsors, and your therapist, you can refine what these early steps must be. After you have selected 10 steps you plan to take, transfer them onto The Systems Transformer (Figure 2.3) on page 68.

1. _____

   _____

   _____

2. _____

   _____

   _____

3. _____

   _____

   _____

4. _____

   _____

   _____

5. _____

   _____

   _____

6. _____

   _____

   _____

7. _____

   _____

   _____

8. _____

   _____

   _____

9. _____

   _____

   _____

10. _____

    _____

    _____

The Systems Transformer

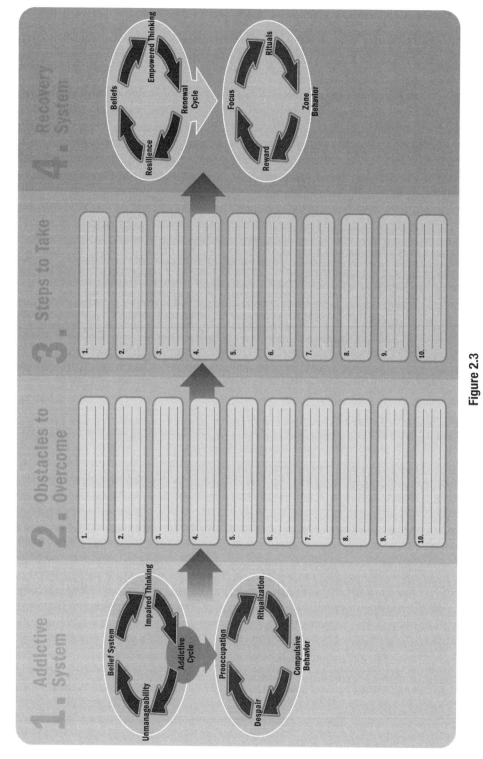

Figure 2.3

How Did I Get This Way?

By this time it must be clear to you whether or not you have a problem. Typical questions emerge with the realization that you do have a problem. You may be wondering why you developed this addiction when others continue to use and drink and have not developed the problem. Following is a brief explanation of the causes of addiction. (See the suggested reading list on page 293 for other sources of information on the origins of addiction.)

- Addicts typically inherit a genetic structure which predisposes them to addictions in general. See Chapter Three for more information.
- Often addicts come from families in which other members suffer from addictions. Parents, siblings, and extended family members will have types of addictive and compulsive behaviors. This increases the probability of actually acquiring addictive behaviors through modeling, family dysfunction, and child abuse, all of which can contribute to the development of addiction.
- Childhood abuse is a factor for many, leading to extreme reactivity or hypersensitivity to pain and emotional upset. When people have difficulties coping with childhood abuse, some will choose to medicate their pain with drugs and alcohol, and this can precipitate development of addiction.
- Depression, anxiety, or other mental illnesses frequently accompany addiction. Feelings of despair intensify addictions and obsessions. For many they begin to use in an attempt to make themselves feel better. This can intensify the mental illness and addiction.
- High stress situations such as medical school, certain careers, or danger such as warfare can perpetuate addiction when there are no other predisposing factors. Traumatic situations such as rape or major medical problems can cause stress so severe and so difficult to cope with that medicating with drugs or alcohol can seem like the only hope for relief.
- Other addictions can also precipitate an addictive pattern. Addictions can actually migrate from one form to another. For example, someone with compulsive overeating behavior might get binge eating under control only to slide into compulsive drinking behaviors.

It will take you some time to understand how you acquired your addiction. In order to start making change, you simply have to start with the fact that you do have an addiction problem. The upcoming chapters will help to further your understanding. Just recognizing that you have a problem is a major step and the beginning to recovery. It requires commitment to take each new step.

The Making of an Addict

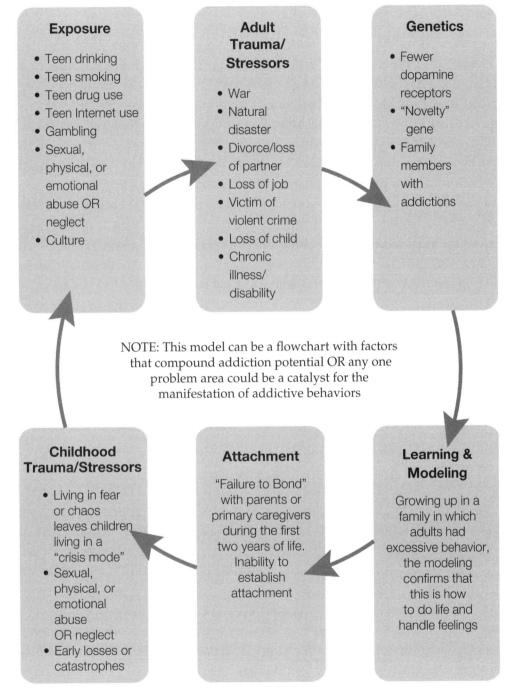

Exposure

- Teen drinking
- Teen smoking
- Teen drug use
- Teen Internet use
- Gambling
- Sexual, physical, or emotional abuse OR neglect
- Culture

Adult Trauma/ Stressors

- War
- Natural disaster
- Divorce/loss of partner
- Loss of job
- Victim of violent crime
- Loss of child
- Chronic illness/ disability

Genetics

- Fewer dopamine receptors
- "Novelty" gene
- Family members with addictions

NOTE: This model can be a flowchart with factors that compound addiction potential OR any one problem area could be a catalyst for the manifestation of addictive behaviors

Childhood Trauma/Stressors

- Living in fear or chaos leaves children living in a "crisis mode"
- Sexual, physical, or emotional abuse OR neglect
- Early losses or catastrophes

Attachment

"Failure to Bond" with parents or primary caregivers during the first two years of life. Inability to establish attachment

Learning & Modeling

Growing up in a family in which adults had excessive behavior, the modeling confirms that this is how to do life and handle feelings

Figure 2.4

Is There Hope for Addicts?

Do addicts ever really recover? Absolutely! There are joyous addicts all over the world who have gotten their lives back and conquered addictions. Just as with other chronic diseases, such as diabetes, addiction is a debilitating illness. However, diabetics can learn how to eat appropriately, manage their weight, and watch for signs of blood sugar problems; this allows them to live and thrive with diabetes. Likewise, addicts can learn how to live and thrive too while managing chemical dependency.

Addicts can have a happy and free life as long as they maintain the processes essential to recovery. Addiction is like a degenerative muscle condition in which you have to exercise your muscles for the rest of your life. Addicts must learn to exercise healthy behaviors for the rest of their lives. This workbook is built on that proven premise. The last chapter of this workbook provides more information about how this program works by creating an overview of the steps that successful recovering people have taken to live in ways that sustain their recovery.

Some people in early recovery find their problems are too overwhelming and see no hope. They keep relapsing, or they become so hopeless and despairing that they consider suicide. Here again, the problem is not hopeless. What these people often need is more support, such as an inpatient (residential) treatment or an outpatient (nonresidential) program. If they are already in therapy, they may need a more structured outpatient program with more frequent appointments and group therapy.

Is Outpatient or Inpatient Therapy Best for You?

A residential program creates a more focused and supportive environment for developing skills for success. The typical program lasts thirty to ninety days (or even longer) and is recommended for those who can't stay sober in an outpatient setting. Usually patients with a longer length of stay have a reduced relapse rate.

If you can develop your skills in the community in which you live, then an outpatient program may be for you. These programs typically include several groups per week, regular attendance at Twelve Step groups, and individual and family therapy. Outpatient programs work best if the recovering person can stay relapse free, has very strong family support, and is committed to the process. It may be helpful to enroll in a monitoring program as part of your recovery that does random drug testing to assist with accountability.

The bottom line is that hope is connected to your motivation. In order to change, you must confront the denial and delusion of your addiction. This can be very difficult and painful and can call into question everything you believe about life and yourself.

At a later point, we will talk in depth about specific steps you can take to jump-start your recovery. For now it is important to learn to have compassion for yourself. Remember that you are not alone. Congratulations on your choice to get your life back.

Chapter Three: **What Is an Addiction?**
Understanding What Has Happened to Your Brain

…becoming addicted is a developmental process. You don't wake up one morning to discover addiction on your skin like a rash you caught unsuspectingly …. No, addiction develops over time, and it involves not only changes in the way you behave but also changes in the way you think….
—from A Place Called Self, *by Stephanie Brown, Ph.D.*

Over the last decade great advances have been made in understanding the human brain. Scientists have learned that the brain grows a multitude of cells very quickly in the first years of life, and then it pares back cells that are not used. Scientists have learned that the cells and circuits that young children use repeatedly grow robustly, and that people can generate new brain cells through the entire lifespan, even after the brain has been damaged by drug and alcohol addiction. Using substances causes damage to your body and your brain, but it is important to know that your brain can heal with prolonged recovery. This chapter will help you understand the damage caused by addiction and how your brain can heal.

With the increasing sophistication of research tools, it has become clear that addiction is a disease of the brain. Scientists use radiologic scans to see what is happening inside the brain. Studies using these tools show that the brain is really changed, chemically and structurally, when a person has become addicted.

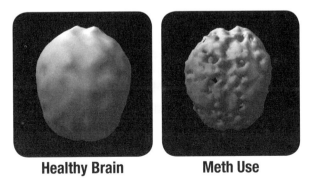

Healthy Brain   **Meth Use**

Figure 3.1

This change doesn't happen all at once. It takes place over time. The brain releases chemicals in our body that reward us, making us feel good when we do certain things such as eating good food, having sex, or drinking alcohol. When we repeat behaviors obsessively to get this reward, we change the way our brain works, the amounts and kinds of chemicals the brain releases, the way the parts of the brain communicate with each other, and even the relative sizes of brain structures.

Addicts, when they are lonely, stressed, or depressed, seek the brain's reward chemicals through certain behaviors or using certain drugs. They feel better temporarily. When they are stressed or lonely again, they use drugs to trigger the pleasure chemical again. The addiction solution works through continuous stimulation. Pleasure can obliterate pain, numb loneliness, and help diminish shame. Eventually, this continuous stimulation actually changes the way the brain works.

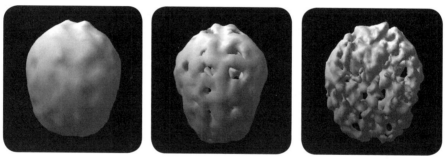

Healthy Brain   **Cocaine Use**   **Heroin Use**

Figure 3.2

Addiction as a Brain Disease

It is important that you understand how the addicted brain has been changed and how it works. It will help you understand how your response to alcohol and drugs has changed and how your cravings get triggered. Knowing how such a change happens can profoundly affect your ability to remain relapse free.

Defining Addiction

The American Society of Addiction Medicine (ASAM) says addiction "is a primary, chronic, neurobiological disease, with genetic, psychosocial, and environmental factors influencing its development and manifestations. It is characterized by behaviors that include one or more of the following: impaired control over drug use, compulsive use, continued use despite harm, and craving." You can find more information on the medical aspects of addiction on ASAM's web site at www.asam.org.

In other words, addiction is a disease of the brain with many causes that result in out-of-control behavior that must be treated. Addicts often have other problems that influence their repeated use, problems like anxiety or depression or painful memories. These are called coexisting conditions. You hear about people using alcohol or drugs to self-medicate to relieve their anxiety or depression. But once an addiction has been developed, you can't just treat the anxiety or depression and expect the addiction to go away. You have to also treat the disease of addiction itself.

ASAM makes the point that addiction is a chronic disease. Like childhood onset diabetes, it is a lifelong condition that requires daily management, in other words an ongoing recovery program. Likewise, there is no cure for addiction and it lasts forever. Addiction can be brought into remission and controlled on a one-day-at-a-time basis. Keep in mind that addiction can always be awakened by using a drug, taking a drink, or ignoring your recovery program.

Many people confuse physical dependence with addiction. You can be addicted even when you are not physically dependent. Many addictive drugs such as alcohol, narcotics used to treat pain, and benzodiazepines used to treat anxiety produce symptoms such as nausea, vomiting, diarrhea, and anxiety when abruptly discontinued. On the other hand, others drugs such as crack cocaine and methamphetamine produce none of these classic withdrawal symptoms when stopped.

Changes in the Brain

Over time addictive drugs change the brain, sometimes quickly, sometimes slowly depending on which drug is used, how it is used, the amount used, and who is using it.

Some people seem to be more vulnerable to developing addiction than others. There is often a strong genetic component. You will remember Jim from the last chapter whose father was an alcoholic. As was the case with Jim, addiction can often be seen running in families. The genetic component has been demonstrated in animal studies. Though most animals will self-administer reinforcing drugs (drugs that trigger pleasure), they can be bred to do it more avidly. In fact, breeding can even produce rats that will accept a shock if they can get the drug at the same time. In other words, these addicted rats take drugs despite negative consequences.

Difficult life situations such as abuse, trauma, and even chronic stress can produce brain changes that make people more susceptible to addiction, adding to the effects of heredity or replacing them altogether. We talked about Kathy in the last chapter. She grew up in a home where her father abused her mother, and Kathy worried all the time about protecting her mother. Although we don't have a scan of Kathy's brain, it is likely that if we did, it would show that the abuse and chronic stress in her home had produced brain changes that made her more vulnerable to developing an addiction.

The nature of the drug, how long it is used, and how it is taken seem to influence the brain changes that produce addictive behavior. Some drugs, such as alcohol may take a long time and heavy use to produce addiction, though the amount and duration required are influenced by genetics and life events. Other drugs, especially those that are inhaled or injected such as crack cocaine, methamphetamine, or tobacco seem to change the brain even with relatively short-term use. It took years of increasingly heavy use for Jim to become addicted to alcohol. Kathy's addiction to crack cocaine occurred much more quickly, because crack's reward is so immediate and so strong. Smoking crack meant that Kathy's brain released dopamine almost immediately and in larger quantities than Jim's brain did in response to alcohol.

How the Brain Works

The brain releases "pleasure chemicals" to reward people for activities that are necessary for survival. Dopamine is one of these chemicals. Food, water, sex, and nurturing all increase dopamine. The dopamine activates brain circuits, also called neuropathways, that let us function. These pathways are the trails along which the neurons in the various structures inside our brains travel to connect with each other. Activity in the brain circuit that tells us to eat is triggered by our desire for dopamine. "Pleasure chemicals" like dopamine spur our basic drives.

Other parts of the brain serve to restrain these basic drives when they are destructive or inappropriate. We have control mechanisms that are constantly evaluating stimuli and the appropriateness of the planned response, applying the brakes when needed. For instance, the part of our brain called the frontal cortex, the rational part of our brain, will tell us we need to stop eating now or we will soon feel uncomfortable. It will tell us to calm down after being startled by something that can't really hurt us. It will tell us to that even though we are attracted to a stranger sitting on seat bus next to us, the negative consequences with our spouse would outweigh the pleasure. The brain's control mechanisms restrain our basic drives when they drive us too far or in the wrong direction.

Addictive substances affect the brain circuitry, and abuse eventually impairs the control mechanisms. Like food or nurturing hugs, addictive substances increase dopamine, but they do it better and faster than natural rewards do. People who are more susceptible to addiction seem to have a lower baseline level of dopamine. They also have a decreased activity in the "restraining" parts of the brain. This can happen because people are born that way (genetics) or because they have been exposed to difficult life events (trauma, chronic stress, and so on), or both. Scientists believe that the brains of people who are predisposed to addiction attribute more survival value to the substances and don't exercise as much restraint, even in the face of consequences.

During a craving, the areas of the brain that create drives are activated while the areas that restrain these urges are deactivated. The result is a person who can't defend against the craving. This all happens at a subconscious level. It is essentially a highjacking of the rational part of the brain. The highjacking is why willpower is virtually useless. There often comes a point during a craving where the addict simply gives in. At this point many addicts will describe a surreal state where they are almost in a trance watching themselves repeat self-destructive behavior.

Denial and magical thinking are thought to be a result of this hijacking. An example of this is found in Chapter Three of *Alcoholic Anonymous*, otherwise known as the Big Book, where the abstinent salesman suddenly decided it was a good idea to go to a bar and have a sandwich and a glass of milk. This was followed by the sudden thought that adding whiskey to the milk was a good idea, and he did so. This is what Jim experienced when he found himself walking into the bar even though he knew it would make him late for his son's Boy Scout activities. He knew his drinking would affect his driving, but his brain had been hijacked; he told himself he could hold his liquor well enough to drive under the influence, even with his son in the car.

It is important to remember that, though lying, stealing, and cheating frequently accompany addictive behavior, most addicts are not true sociopaths. They feel guilt and shame over their inexplicable behavior, and self-medication of these feelings may be another driving force in drug and alcohol use.

Long-term Changes

Finally, the chronic surges of dopamine produced by drugs and alcohol cause the brain's own dopamine "factory" to shut down. Those suffering from addiction lose the ability to enjoy activities that they previously found pleasurable. People short of dopamine have difficulty feeling joy. Relationships fall apart, hobbies and athletic activities cease, and often addicts withdraw from the world into a state of despair and isolation. At this point addicts do not get high or feel euphoria. Instead, drugs elevate their mood to a level that is often slightly above suicidal. Despair and shame can be so great that suicide is a significant risk. However, during this state of what the Big Book calls "incomprehensible demoralization" addicts are often at their bottom, and having no other choice, they may be receptive to help.

Permanent Changes

Some changes in the brain are permanent. The addicted brain on some level will always crave the dopamine that it knows drugs can provide. Animal and human studies have shown that all addictive drugs can "wake up" the reward centers and deactivate control centers. This means that even drugs in a different class can trigger cravings and relapse. Many addicts have relapsed because they believe enough time has passed for them to return to controlled use or because they believe they can safely use a different class of drugs. For instance, Jim entered a treatment program and was abstinent for ten years. He was at a party with old friends who were smoking marijuana and he thought it was no big deal to join them. After all, it was alcohol that had gotten him into trouble. But the dopamine increase from marijuana triggered a powerful craving in him for alcohol. Fortunately, he was in close touch with his sponsor and was able to disrupt the cycle before he relapsed.

Effects on the Body

Many addictive drugs also have destructive effects on your body. Alcohol may be the most physically destructive. It causes memory and reasoning problems that are similar to Alzheimer's disease. It can cause various cancers, nerve damage, and liver cirrhosis, which may be fatal. Withdrawal from alcohol can also be fatal and must be carefully managed. Other drugs cause serious damage to the body as well. Addicts may get hepatitis and HIV when they inject heroine. Both marijuana and cocaine can result in psychosis. There are many other damaging effects from addictive substances. Figure 3.3 on pages 82–85 shows some of these effects.

Effects on the Body

	Alcohol	Sedative	Stimulants	Opioids	Marijuana	LSD	Inhalants	Anabolic Steroids	Ecstasy	Tobacco
Addiction	X	X	X	X	X		X	X	X	
Life threatening withdrawal	X	X		X						
BRAIN										
Decreased memory	X	X	X		X	X	X		X	
Brain shrinkage	X				X	X	X			
Decreased reasoning	X	X	X	X	X	X	X		X	
Decreased problem solving	X	X		X	X	X	X			
Dementia	X						X			
Long-term brain damage	X					X	X		X	
EMOTIONAL/BEHAVIORAL										
Psychosis	X	X	X		X	X	X	X	X	
Depression	X	X	X	X			X	X	X	
Anxiety			X		X	X	X		X	
Emotional Instability	X	X	X				X	X	X	
Flashbacks						X				
Traumatic hallucinations/illusions	X	X	X		X	X	X		X	
Sleep disorders or Insomnia	X	X	X			X			X	

Figure 3.3

Effects on the Body continued

	Alcohol	Sedative	Stimulants	Opioids	Marijuana	LSD	Inhalants	Anabolic Steroids	Ecstasy	Tobacco
Decreased motivation	X	X		X	X					
Risk-taking behaviors	X	X	X			X		X	X	X
Impaired judgment	X	X	X	X	X	X	X	X	X	X
Accidents, falls	X	X		X	X	X	X			
Decreased reaction time	X			X	X					
Decreased coordination	X	X		X	X		X	X		
Exacerbation of mental disorders	X	X	X	X	X	X	X	X	X	
Anger	X		X			X	X	X		
Risky sexual behaviors	X		X						X	
CANCERS										
Mouth	X									X
Throat	X									X
Pancreatic	X									X
Liver	X							X		
Stomach	X									X
Larynx	X									X
Tracheae	X									X
Lung			X				X			X
Esophagus	X									X

Figure 3.3

Effects on the Body continued

	Alcohol	Sedative	Stimulants	Opioids	Marijuana	LSD	Inhalants	Anabolic Steroids	Ecstasy	Tobacco
OTHER PHYSICAL PROBLEMS										
Liver problems	X	X	X	X			X	X	X	
Seizures	X		X	X			X		X	
Nerve damage	X						X		X	
Neuropathies	X						X		X	
Lung and respiratory	X		X		X		X			X
Respiratory depression	X	X		X	X		X			X
Heart attack or heart-related problems	X		X		X		X	X	X	X
Testicular atrophy	X			X	X			X		
Anemia	X						X			
Stroke	X		X					X		X
Pancreatitis	X									
Ulcers	X									
Infection (decreased immunity)	X							X		
Birth defects	X	X	X	X			X	X	X	X
Cataracts	X									
Hepatitis (with injection)			X	X						

Figure 3.3

Facing Addiction: Starting Recovery from Alcohol and Drugs

Effects on the Body continued

	Alcohol	Sedative	Stimulants	Opioids	Marijuana	LSD	Inhalants	Anabolic Steroids	Ecstasy	Tobacco
Increased body temperature						X			X	
Jaw pain, dental problems, nasal septum erosion, or nose bleeds			X						X	
Conjunctival hemorrhage			X							
Fetal cleft palate		X								
Increased blood sugar Diabetes, unwanted hair growth, and acne									X	
Weight gain	X				X					
Constipation				X						

Figure 3.3

Worksheet 3.1: **Brain Damage Map**

Directions: If you have used drugs and alcohol chronically, it may have had a long-term impact on your brain. Below, circle the substances on the brain map that you use. Then trace the lines from those substances to the brain to see what parts of your brain may have been damaged.

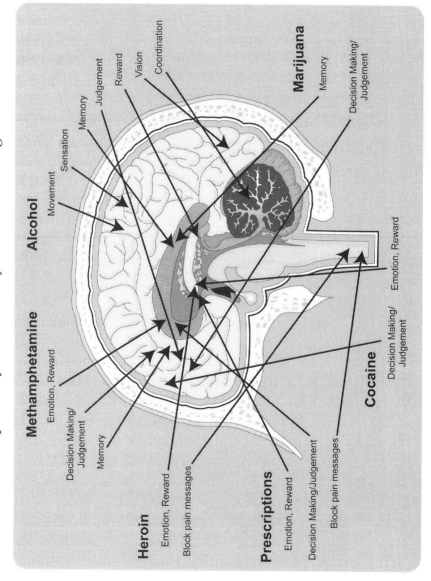

Methamphetamine

Emotion, Reward

Decision Making/
Judgement

Memory

Heroin

Emotion, Reward

Block pain messages

Prescriptions

Emotion, Reward

Decision Making/Judgement

Block pain messages

Alcohol

Movement

Sensation

Memory

Judgement

Reward

Vision

Coordination

Marijuana

Memory

Decision Making/
Judgement

Cocaine

Decision Making/
Judgement

Emotion, Reward

Brain Healing

As you begin your recovery your body must adjust to the absence of the chemicals it is used to having all the time. This process, called detoxification, must be carefully monitored by a health care professional because your body may have strong reactions to the sudden absence of some drugs or alcohol. For instance, withdrawal of alcohol from a body that is used to having it all the time can produce seizures. Medications such as tranquilizers can help ease the detox process, but they should be managed by someone who specializes in addiction medicine.

After drug detoxification, it takes a while for the brain to heal and for the "dopamine factory" to rebuild. During this time of healing, many people experience symptoms that are referred to as *post-acute withdrawal*. These are symptoms such as difficulty sleeping, depression, anxiety, difficulty concentrating, and disturbing "using dreams." These are difficult symptoms to live with. Those who are going through this need encouragement and constant reminding since this can last a long time—as long as twelve to eighteen months. It can help you cope with these symptoms if you take time to identify them. Being aware of what is happening in your body can take the mystery away and lessen the misery.

Worksheet 3.2: **Post-acute Withdrawal Symptoms (PAWS)**

Directions: Check the post-acute withdrawal symptoms that you are experiencing below.

Cognitive symptoms of PAWS

_____ I have racing or recycling thoughts.

_____ My thoughts are scattered.

_____ Others notice a certain rigidity of thinking and lack of required flexibility in me.

_____ I sometimes have difficulty understanding cause and effect.

_____ I have difficulty concentrating and paying attention.

_____ I sometimes experience confusion.

_____ I have difficulty prioritizing.

_____ I am too emotional.

_____ I make mountains out of molehills.

_____ I feel shame a lot of the time.

_____ I have trouble feeling anything, like I am numb.

_____ My inability to feel hurts my relationships.

_____ I have short-term memory problems.

_____ I have more difficulty learning than I did before I began using.

_____ I don't remember much from when I was a child.

It may be appropriate to treat some of the post-acute withdrawal symptoms you checked on Worksheet 3.2 (page 88) with medication, but it is important to avoid addictive drugs. These symptoms can mimic sleep disorders, depression, anxiety, or attention-deficit hyperactivity disorder (ADHD), which are all sometimes treated with addictive medications. These include benzodiazepines (such as Xanax, Librium, Valium, Ativan), or methylphenidate and amphetamine (such as Ritalin, Concerta, Metadate). These medications may be appropriate for people who are not addicts. However, these drugs can trigger relapse and prolong or reverse natural healing for addicts. It is important to consult an addiction medical specialist who can guide appropriate medical management of your addiction treatment. This is especially important when confronted with unexpected life events that may require pain medication such as the need for surgery.

Promoting a Healthy Brain and Body

Many of the long-term harmful effects of drugs improve with time. For example, memory and reasoning ability will improve. Breathing problems from cigarettes may stabilize and improve, and the likelihood of developing lung cancer decreases. The liver, one of the most remarkable regenerative organs in the body, if not taken past the point of no return often improves to normal function. Circulation to the heart, organs, and limbs will also improve with abstinence. However, there can be permanent effects, so the sooner one gets into recovery, the better.

Research suggests that there are lifestyle changes and activities that can help trigger or accelerate repair of the damage induced by drug use. Examples of these include exercise, good nutrition, restorative sleep, healthy relationships, and in some cases psychotherapy.

It is also important to see a physician for a complete physical and to see a mental health professional for a psychological or psychiatric assessment as you travel the recovery road. They can determine if there are specific problems that you need to attend to and help you decide on necessary treatments.

Exercise

One of the most powerful and effective healing "medications" is exercise. Up until recently, it was believed that most of the positive effects of exercise were due to increases in endorphins. While this is true, the effects of exercise on the brain are even more dramatic than previously believed. For example, animal and human studies suggest that exercise can trigger brain repair, or " neurogenesis," in the hippocampus and prefrontal cortex, areas that are affected by chronic drug use, psychological trauma, or chronic stress. In fact, symptoms of depression, post-acute withdrawal, Post-Traumatic Stress Disorder (PTSD), and decreased memory can respond dramatically. Exercise can also counter the weight gain that often occurs in early recovery as the brain looks to replace dopamine from drugs with dopamine from food. Activities that require mental activity or sustained concentration such as reading, crossword puzzles, video games, playing a musical instrument, or yoga may also have positive effects.

Nutrition

Those suffering from addiction tend to neglect themselves, and malnutrition is common. Good nutrition and a balanced diet, and in many cases a vitamin supplement, can be helpful, both to restore deficits as well as to provide the substances used in brain and body healing. This is especially important with alcohol, which depletes important nutrients including folate, thiamine, potassium and calcium.

Sleep

Much of the physical and brain repair occurs during sleep. The extremely important phase of sleep known as REM is suppressed by many addictive drugs, and catching up can take some time.

Healthy Relationships

Addiction is a disease of isolation. Being socially active—being involved with recovery friends, volunteering, having the support of family and friends—is a part of an effective recovery program. Recovery friends and a sponsor can increase accountability. They can also provide motivation, guidance, and help spot denial and the destructive "stinking thinking" that occurs with addiction. Furthermore, interaction with others, love, and nurturing may also play a role in brain repair.

Psychotherapy

Therapy helps you understand how your choices have contributed to your problems and supports your positive behavioral changes. Therapy may also promote brain healing. There is evidence that effective psychotherapy may trigger changes in gene expression and neurogenesis, producing effects on the brain similar to those of antidepressants. Furthermore, when you react with new feelings and behaviors, you change the pathways used by the parts of your brain to connect with each other. The more you practice your new responses and behaviors, the stronger the new pathways become.

While each of these activities makes its own contribution to brain healing, the activities become very powerful in combination. Taken together, they form a holistic approach to healing. It is important to make space in your life to care for your physical, mental, emotional, and spiritual needs. You will often hear addiction spoken of as a disease of the mind, body, and soul, and recovery requires a lifestyle balanced among all of these areas.

Recovery

Here is an overview of the elements of a good recovery program and the barriers to recovery. We will be looking at these more closely in the rest of this book.

Recovery is a one-day-at-a-time process and requires a lifelong commitment. The risk that the reward-seeking part of your brain will be re-engaged and cause cravings will exist for the rest of your life. Whether it's after two years of abstinence or twenty years of abstinence, you may still be vulnerable to cravings. The good news is that after a period of abstinence, the likelihood of the rational brain being hijacked by the addicted brain diminishes somewhat. A healthy lifestyle and good recovery program can reduce the likelihood of this occurring. The following two pages show an overview of the elements of a good recovery program and the barriers to recovery.

Elements of a Good Recovery Program

- **Avoid all drug use.** Animal and human studies have shown that all addictive drugs can "wake up" the reward centers and deactivate control centers. Thus, even drugs in a different class can trigger cravings and relapse. Addiction is a permanent brain change. Many addicts have relapsed due to the belief that enough time has passed for them to return to controlled use.

- **Avoid or learn to cope with "people, places, and things" that trigger alcohol or drug use.** Environments associated with past use can bring back cravings.

- **Attend meetings where you can get support.** Twelve Step groups allow you to reflect on and tell your own story while listening to other's stories. It is important to look for similarities when comparing your story with others rather than focusing on differences. Rationalizations, comparisons with others, and impaired thinking may be the subconscious workings of the mind intent on obtaining the dopamine it perceives as necessary for survival.

- **Use a sponsor.** A sponsor can help the recovering addict work the Twelve Steps, challenge self-defeating thoughts, and keep denial at bay.

- **Work the Twelve Steps.** Working on distortions in thinking, self-defeating character flaws, guilt, shame, resentments, lack of hope and broken relationships are all absolutely necessary to avoid future relapses. As is often heard in recovery programs, "Recovery is easy…just change everything."

- **Address depression, sleep disorders, anxiety, personal stress, and chronic pain, since all of these can trigger relapse.** Therapy is critical to helping you address these problems, and medication may be helpful as well. However, it is important to work with a specialist in addiction medicine since many medications used to address these problems can trigger relapse.

- **Engage in healthy passions and enjoyable activities.** A low baseline of dopamine may have produced addiction vulnerability. It is dangerous to ignore this. Enjoyable activities and passions can help to restore dopamine toward normal levels.

Barriers to Recovery

- Belief that you are cured and can return to "responsible use."

- Not understanding cross addiction, that non-preferred drugs, like alcohol can trigger relapse.

- Lack of meeting attendance and involvement.

- Looking for differences rather than similarities with others in meetings.

- Taking prescription medications that are addictive to treat sleep problems, anxiety, or other issues.

- Lack of adequate preparation for life events such as surgery. It is helpful to see a doctor who is a specialist in addiction prior to surgery to discuss medication options.

- Lack of a sponsor and recovery peers who provide support and can spot impaired thinking.

- Not setting boundaries with people, places, and things that can trigger memories and cravings.

- Not controlling stress, depression, anxiety, sleep problems, chronic pain, and other issues.

- Lack of exercise, good nutrition, and engaging in a healthy lifestyle.

- Lack of passions and fun activities.

- Lack of self-care, becoming "hungry, angry, lonely, tired" (HALT).

Chapter Four: **What Is the First Step?**
Accepting the Problem

*The tremendous fact for every one of us is that we have
discovered a common solution.*
—*from* Alcoholics Anonymous, *the Big Book*

Some seventy years ago, a stockbroker who was down on his luck because of his drinking problem sat in the kitchen of a house on Ardmore Street in Akron, Ohio. The house belonged to a physician, Dr. Bob, who had the same problem. He simply could not stop drinking. They sat over a cup of coffee discussing a letter the broker had received from Carl Jung, the famous physician pioneer of psychotherapy. In the letter, Jung told Bill W. that if their new group was to achieve success, they had to pass on their stories. Essentially, the key to success was to help each other as opposed to acting alone.

Thus was born the "telling of the story" that has been the cornerstone of Alcoholics Anonymous. The framework these men developed has helped millions of people. Alcoholics and other people with other addictions have all benefited from their original insights. The key outcome of telling one's story is that the teller admits that he or she has a problem while the listeners affirm the teller by acknowledging that they had the same experience. This transaction reduces the shame for all involved and supports them in their common commitment to stay sober.

Storytelling is powerful. When parents, for example, tell family stories, the children always object if a piece is left out. One might ask why the children want to hear these stories again and again since they already know them so well. The answer is that the storytelling is not about passing on information. It is about bonding. The child feels bonded in that he or she is a part of the story. To return to our earlier discussion about addiction stemming from a failure to bond, Twelve Step groups actually begin a re-bonding process that helps people make up the deficits of the past. Members of a Twelve Step community become accepted for who they are.

Such bonding holds incredible importance, as this additional example illustrates. When Amnesty International first attempted therapy to help torture victims, they got nowhere. Victims of torture, even though they were miserable, resisted help at a most profound level. Eventually, a staff member made a discovery. If torture victims could tell the story of their experience to a room full of other people who were also torture victims, an acceptance of the experience occurred. The victim was then able to bond enough to make therapy succeed. The same happened earlier with drug addiction and alcoholism. Professionals tried to help for years, but it was not until AA provided a format for alcoholics to tell their stories that therapy could actually help. Many addicts have experienced deep trauma in their lives. What's more, being an addict of any type is traumatic in itself. These people need a safe place with other people who share similar experiences.

The Existential Position on Change

Essentially, the storytelling details the way life used to be and how it is today. Put simply, the story is about change. The Twelve Steps, more than anything else, teach about profound change in a person's life. They essentially reveal a life stance—what psychologists and philosophers call an *existential position*—on how to live. The Twelve Steps are actually sound principles about change and life that everyone can use, but they are especially useful for those who have to experience the radical changes of recovery.

The spirit of these principles is best captured in what is called the Serenity Prayer. The Serenity Prayer is credited to Dr. Reinhold Niebuhr and recited at many types of Twelve Step groups. It is reprinted here:

> *God grant me*
> *the serenity to accept the things I cannot change,*
> *courage to change the things I can,*
> *and the wisdom to know the difference.*

The internal acceptance of the ideas expressed in this prayer helps reduce anxiety dramatically. Addictions draw their power from anxiety and fear.

Step One of Alcoholics Anonymous also helps people understand how to begin breaking the grip of addiction on their lives. It reads, "We admitted we were powerless over our addiction—that our lives had become unmanageable." People who do a First Step usually learn the following lessons:

- that you must accept totally that you have a problem
- that you recognize there are things happening you cannot control by yourself
- that to be successful you have to ask for help from others
- that you must focus on what you can do
- that you have to give up secrets and pretending to be something that you are not
- that addictive behaviors will continue until you truly learn this lesson

The following series of worksheets will help you prepare for a First Step. As you work through them, we encourage you to ask for help. A therapist can be a wonderful resource as you think about these issues. You also should select a couple of "consultants" from your Twelve Step group or your therapy group to help you. Whenever you feel shameful or discouraged or unsure about what to do, get a consultation, talk to someone, and ask for help. Remember, this is exactly what those guys did back in Dr. Bob's kitchen.

Worksheet 4.1: **Your Addiction History**

Directions: This section asks you to focus on the development of your alcohol or drug addiction. Because it may be difficult for you to recall specific events or details, respond to the following questions as best you can.

1. At what age do you believe your addiction started (alcohol or drugs helped you to cope; you lost faith in yourself)?

_____

2. What were some critical events during the early development of your addiction (increase in frequency, unmanageability, abandonment, abuse)?

_____

_____

_____

_____

3. At what age do you believe your addiction was firmly established (life priorities became reversed, your preoccupation with drinking or using drugs interfered with your life, job, family?)

_____

4. What were some critical events during this period of your addiction (stressors, denial, impaired thinking)?

_____

_____

_____

_____

5. Were there periods during your life in which your addiction suddenly escalated in terms of frequency of drinking or using drugs?

_____

6. Was there a seasonal (spring, summer, fall, winter) pattern in your use?

_____ Yes   _____ No

If yes, please specify. _____

_____

_____

_____

7. What were some critical events during these periods of escalation?

_____

_____

_____

_____

8. At what ages or time frames do you believe your addiction was at its highest level (for instance, after a traumatic event such as death of a loved one)?

_____

_____

_____

_____

9. What were some critical events that took place during this period when your addiction was at its highest level?

_____

_____

_____

_____

10. Were there periods during your life when your addiction de-escalated (was less intense, went underground, was controlled)?

_____ Yes _____ No

If yes, at what ages? _____

11. What were some critical events that preceded this de-escalation or that occurred during it?

_____

_____

_____

_____

12. Were there periods during your life when it seemed that you had no life beyond the obsession with drugs or alcohol (you had breaks in reality, you completely abandoned your value system)?

_____ Yes _____ No

If yes, at what ages? _____

13. What were some critical events during these periods?

_____

_____

_____

_____

14. Are you currently working on limiting other compulsive behaviors, or are you currently in recovery for any other addiction?

_____ Yes   _____ No

These include:
- compulsive use of another drug
- codependency
- eating disorders (overeating, anorexia, bulimia)
- nicotine/tobacco addiction
- caffeine abuse or addiction
- compulsive gambling
- compulsive spending
- compulsive work
- compulsive sexual acting out
- relationship addiction
- other, specify: _____

15. How did your other addictions (if any) affect your addiction to alcohol or drugs?

_____

_____

_____

_____

Worksheet 4.2: **Powerlessness Inventory**

Directions: List thirty examples showing how powerless you have been to stop your behavior. Remember, powerless means being unable to stop the behavior despite obvious consequences. Be very explicit about types of behavior and frequency. Start with your earliest example of being powerless, and conclude with the most recent. By generating as many examples as possible, you will have added significantly to the depth of your understanding of your own powerlessness. You do not have to complete the list in one sitting. Add to the list as examples occur to you. When you finish this inventory, do not proceed until you have discussed it with one of your "guides," such as a therapist, sponsor, or someone else in recovery. You deserve support with each piece of significant work.

Example: My wife told me she would leave me if I drank again, and I did it anyway.

1. _____

   _____

2. _____

   _____

3. _____

   _____

4. _____

   _____

5. _____

   _____

6. _____

   _____

7. _____

   _____

8. _____

   _____

9. _____

   _____

10. _____

    _____

11. _____

    _____

12. _____

    _____

13. _____

_____

14. _____

_____

15. _____

_____

16. _____

_____

17. _____

_____

18. _____

_____

19. _____

_____

20. _____

_____

21. _____

_____

22. _____

_____

23. _____

_____

24. _____

_____

25. _____

_____

26. _____

_____

27. _____

_____

28. _____

_____

29. _____

_____

30. _____

_____

The most recent examples will make you feel your powerlessness most strongly. Circle five recent examples.

Unmanageability Inventory

Here are examples of how some people said their lives had become un-manageable:

- People were lying for me at work to cover for my absences.
- Had two pregnancies in two years, giving up both children for adoption.
- Realized that hangovers were seriously affecting my work.
- Lost three marriages, all because of my drinking.
- Spent money on drugs when I needed it for my children's clothes.
- Didn't know which man was the father of my child.
- Stayed in my marriage despite physical abuse.
- Went to bars during work time.
- Lost promotion opportunities and a scholarship because coworkers discovered my drug use.
- Stayed out all night and slept all day despite kids to care for.

Worksheet 4.3: **Unmanageability Inventory**

Directions: List as many examples as you can that show how your life has become totally unmanageable because of your addiction. Remember, *unmanageability* means that your addiction created chaos and damage in your life.

     If you need further ideas, return to Chapter One and review your list of consequences on pages 23–25. Again, when you finish this inventory, stop and talk to your guides. You deserve support. At the end of the worksheet you will be asked to identify recent examples of unmanageability.

Example: Got caught stealing two years ago to support my addiction.

1. _____

2. _____

3. _____

4. _____

5. _____

6. _____

7. _____

8. _____

9. _____

10. _____

11. _____

12. _____

13. _____

14. _____

15. _____

16. _____

17. _____

18. _____

19. _____

20. _____

21. _____

22. _____

23. _____

24. _____

25. _____

26. _____

27. _____

28. _____

29. _____

30. _____

The most recent examples will make you feel your unmanage-ability most strongly. Circle five that have happened to you in the last ten days. Circle another five that have happened to you during the past thirty days.

Financial Costs

Alcohol and drug addiction can be very expensive. The cost of the drug itself or the increasing costs of more and more alcohol, medical costs, divorces, and lost businesses are just a few of the ways addicts pay a price for their addiction. Many addicts hit a point of no return when they add up just the financial costs of their use and associated behavior. Usually the financial costs in no way approach the emotional and personal costs. Yet determining how much of your resources have gone into your use provides a clear index of how out of control you have been. For many, totaling up the bill is staggering because they have substantially deluded themselves about the costs. Most addicts spent more than they could afford.

Worksheet 4.4: **Financial Costs**

Directions: The following worksheet will help you determine what the financial costs of your addiction are. Go through each section carefully and total each. You may have to use separate sheets of paper to make the calculations. Enter the description and provide your best estimate as to how much you have spent. Some of the costs may have to be approximate. The goal is to document what has happened to you, not to survive an audit. You know more than anyone what the costs have been. Simply record what those costs probably were. Use your consultants if you are stuck or need support.

Direct Spending

Include money spent on alcohol and drugs, paraphernalia, or venues for using such as bars or concerts.

Item Amount Total $ _____

Business and Career Costs

Include lost earning time and lawsuits for inappropriate behavior. Consider costs due to bad performance or bad decisions because you were using. If a career has been lost or suspended, include the cost of training and what income has been lost. If a business has been lost, calculate not only the investment, but what potential earnings were lost. Include the misuse of other people's money, hush money, and bail money for self or others.

Item Amount Total $ _____

Medical Expenses

Include obvious direct expenses such as treatment for alcoholism, liver disease, HIV, hepatitis, or other diseases transmitted by contaminated syringes, or severe dental problems. Specify medical costs for car accidents or other accidents that occurred while under the influence of drugs or alcohol. If major medical conditions occurred, such as a heart attack due to behaviors resulting from alcohol or drug use, specify that as well.

Item Amount Total $ _____

Divorce or Family Support

Include divorce costs including attorney fees, child support, and settlements. Specify any ongoing payments to those for whom you have felt guilt or have been legally required to support.

Item Amount Total $ _____

Legal Problems

Include money spent on attorneys for defense against legal charges, bail money, and court fees. Consider lost time due to legal involvements, prison stays, or workhouse sentences. Any lawsuit not part of your business or career but a result of your using behavior should be recorded.

Item Amount Total $ _____

Add up all the total costs here $ _____

Reflection on the total

What insights or reflections do you have now that you see an approximate cost? If that money was available to you today, what would you be able to do with it? What role has money played for you in this process? Records your thoughts below:

_____

_____

_____

_____

_____

_____

_____

_____

_____

_____

_____

_____

_____

Give five examples of denial about your spending. *Example: I was always short of cash at the end of the month but never saw it as a result of my alcohol or drug use.*

1. _____

_____

_____

2. _____

_____

_____

3. _____

_____

_____

4. _____

_____

_____

5. _____

_____

_____

Give five examples of delusion (rationalization and justification) about your spending. *Example: I told myself I would do my work better if I got high.*

1. _____

_____

_____

2. _____

_____

_____

3. _____

_____

_____

4. _____

_____

_____

5. _____

_____

_____

Record your reactions to your denial or delusions about the costs of your addiction. Start with your thoughts and then record your feelings. *Example: I thought my divorce settlement was unfair. I feel that my ex-spouse is still punishing me.*

Thoughts:_____

_____

_____

_____

_____

_____

Feelings:_____

_____

_____

_____

_____

_____

_____

Worksheet 4.5: **Ten Worst Moments**

Directions: List your ten worst moments as an alcoholic or drug addict. Think of events that were the most painful or catastrophic. For each event, record the feelings you had then and the feelings you have now as you look back on these moments.

1. Worst moment: _____

_____

_____

_____

Feelings then: _____

Feelings now: _____

2. Worst moment: _____

_____

_____

_____

Feelings then: _____

Feelings now: _____

3. Worst moment: _____

_____

_____

_____

Feelings then: _____

Feelings now: _____

4. Worst moment: _____

_____

_____

_____

Feelings then: _____

Feelings now: _____

5. Worst moment: _____

_____

_____

_____

Feelings then: _____

Feelings now: _____

6. Worst moment: _____

_____

_____

_____

Feelings then: _____

Feelings now: _____

7. Worst moment: _____

_____

_____

_____

Feelings then: _____

Feelings now: _____

8. Worst moment: _____

_____

_____

_____

Feelings then: _____

Feelings now: _____

9. Worst moment: _____

_____

_____

_____

Feelings then: _____

Feelings now: _____

10. Worst moment: _____

_____

_____

_____

Feelings then: _____

Feelings now: _____

Now that you have completed the list, rank the worst moments by putting a "1" next to the worst, a "2" next to the second worst, and continue until you have ranked all 10. This will help you focus on what you will share in your First Step process.

Sharing Your First Step

You will share your First Step many times. Initially, it will be with your Twelve Step groups and in therapy. As you progress, you will share in other groups, with sponsors, and with those you love. This will be the part of your story about how bad it was. As we noted earlier, this "retelling the story" is not about reporting the facts. Rather it is done to create the sincere bond that comes out of deep sharing. We have noted how telling the story teaches principles about change. As you make "multiple presentations," a life stance emerges about change and stress. This chapter and the next are designed to help you understand that "stance."

The First Step also breaks rules about always looking good and keeping secrets, and thus it helps destroy the secret life and the shame that perpetuates dishonesty. As that happens, addicts start to experience long-buried feelings. Obliterated and numbed by your obsession and behavior, these feelings have haunted your life. As you share your story, you will also be able to share your feelings. Not only is this important self-knowledge, but expressing these feelings will allow others to know your interior world. Those who listen can then provide feedback and support. That exchange is essential to the healing process. In short, you cannot share your First Step without sharing the feelings that go with it. Unexpressed feelings provide fuel for all addictions.

Addicts have years and even decades of practice at ignoring feelings, containing feelings, and hiding feelings, so expressing them is awkward at first. Yet, expressing those feelings is how those who listen will know that you are really internalizing your First Step. A predictable pattern exists. It typically goes as follows:

- Defensive explanation and manipulation—indicates addict is still in denial
- Reporting the facts—shows intellectual understanding
- Expressions of anger and fear—reflects addict taking responsibility
- Describing shame and embarrassment—means addictive pride lifts
- Sharing sadness and pain—shows emotional understanding
- Admits depth of loneliness—indicates acceptance

Reaching the point of acceptance represents a profound turning point for most people in recovery. Here are some tips on how to get there. There should be two people from your group who know the whole story, along with your therapist. With these people, go over all the work that you have done in this workbook, including your use of alcohol or drugs, your behaviors that resulted from your use, your consequences, your examples of powerlessness, your examples of unmanageability, your costs, and your worst moments. When you present your Step, you will not be able to tell the whole story since there usually is a limited amount of group time. Your goal is to share your feelings. If you can get to your core feelings, other people will not need all the details. Focus on the most painful and shameful parts for you. Your guiding question should always be how bad it was for you. Ask your consultants and your therapist for help deciding what parts of your story and feelings to present.

Many addicts find it difficult to feel. Here are some ideas that can help you do so. Select items that involve impact on your children, your spouse or partner's pain, your losses, or your public embarrassment. Ask yourself what would it be like if everyone knew everything. Use your "Ten Worst Moments List" from pages 116–119 to help you access your feelings. Your Twelve Step group or your therapist may ask you to put additional work into it until they see your complete acceptance. Asking you to work on it more is normal. It means two things. First they are supporting you and pushing you to really get your needs met. Second, they know what acceptance looks like. Here is what they look for:

- no excuses or explanations (you behaved the way you did because you behaved the way you did)
- clear understanding of powerlessness, with good examples of efforts to stop
- clear understanding of unmanageability, with good examples of consequences
- knowledge of your own addictive system
- knowledge of how your behavior fit the criteria for addiction
- your worst moments expressed and your secrets exposed
- taking full responsibility for actions
- a range of feelings expressed
- feelings are appropriate for the events reported

- suffering including grief, pain, sorrow, and remorse
- ownership of loneliness
- a commitment to do whatever it takes to change

With those criteria in mind you then tell your story.

Sometimes addicts get confused about how one can be powerless and still take responsibility. A paradox does exist here, but it becomes sound advice if you remember this: Alone you are powerless and you are unable to stop your behavior; however, with help you can change and become responsible. You did the behavior. No one else is responsible for it. You chose your behavior. Now, by knowing what you know, you have a responsibility to use the tools you have and to get the help you need. There were forces at work that you did not understand, but now you have new insights.

Getting Help from a Higher Power

Step Two and Step Three state:

> Came to believe that a Power greater than ourselves could restore us to sanity.

> Made a decision to turn our will and our lives over to the care of God as we *understood Him*.

The idea of a "Power greater than ourselves"—a Higher Power—is a fundamental part of the Twelve Step program. This can be as confusing as the paradox of powerlessness. Sometimes people think the only way to view a Higher Power is the traditional view of God. But Step Three includes the words *as we understood Him*. There are many ways to understand a Higher Power. You may understand a Higher Power as "Her," or as the connection you feel with the universe, or as your Twelve Step group. The point is to recognize that you depend on something bigger than your individual self in recovery and you don't try to control the process yourself.

Sometimes addicts have a lot of trouble believing that any form of a Higher Power exists. When this is the case, you can decide to act "as if," and not worry about whether you *really* believe in a Higher Power." Many people have found that *belief follows action*.

Worksheet 4.6: **Higher Power**

Directions: This worksheet will help you consider your understanding of a Higher Power. Answer the following questions.

1. Do you believe in a Higher Power?

_____ Yes   _____ No

2. If your answer was yes, describe your understanding of a Higher Power.

_____

_____

_____

_____

_____

_____

3. If your answer was no, describe what you would want a Higher Power to be like.

_____

_____

_____

_____

_____

_____

4. Spirituality is the way to help our spirit be "alive and happy." This is the beginning of healing our spirit through a belief in a Higher Power. What are some spiritual things you already do?

_____

_____

_____

_____

_____

_____

_____

5. List the places you have been that made your spirit feel joyfulness, serenity, or wonderment?

_____

_____

_____

_____

_____

_____

_____

6. What things do you do either alone or with others that make your spirit feel alive and joyful?

_____

_____

_____

_____

_____

_____

_____

_____

7. What are your greatest fears about turning your life over to a Higher Power?

_____

_____

_____

_____

_____

_____

_____

Remember the advice from the Big Book of Alcoholics Anonymous when it described addiction as "cunning and powerful." Your "addict" will attempt to sabotage your early step work. Here are some things that might happen:

- You may be tempted to drink or use drugs, even just a little bit.
- You may want to keep a secret or protect someone.
- You may want to procrastinate on telling your story.
- You may find distractions and things to upset you.
- You may find fault with your group, your therapist, or your treatment program.
- You may find or create a family crisis.
- You may find yourself craving in your other addictions.
- You may find yourself mired in self-hatred and self-loathing.

In other words, your "addict" may ask you to stay loyal to the old ways. It is cunning and powerful! Yet, if you persevere, you will find that the Twelve Steps teach a new and more conscious way of life. Anxiety and suffering become guides rather than enemies. You will learn that change is the substance of life and that the unknown is experienced by everybody. That which used to cripple you will become an extraordinary source of wisdom. Troubles will not cease, but your effectiveness will multiply. And you get to have problems that are not the result of drinking or using drugs. You will forge new bonds and be respected for how you handle yourself. No matter how big the fear or the challenge, a sense of peace will pervade all you do. You start by honestly sharing who you are—just like those people back on Ardmore Avenue.

Chapter Five: **What Damage Has Been Done?**
Responding to Change and Crisis

You choose your behavior, but the world chooses your consequences.
—Pat Mellody

The quote above highlights the reality for most addicts that unmanageability may continue long after the recovery. Simply said, addictive behaviors often cause much damage. And addicts have little control over some of those consequences. Pat Mellody uses this phrase to remind addicts who are angry about how things are unraveling that their behavior brought on all these problems. This is a difficult moment for people who now realize they have an addiction and are working hard at recovery—but the problems continue. To them, this does not seem fair.

This chapter focuses on helping you face consequences using recovery principles. In early recovery, life usually seems to be spinning out of control. Arrests, health issues, job problems, money difficulties, and family complications all add up. Early recovery is hard, especially if you are out of work or fighting the AIDS virus or your partner has initiated divorce. It is typical to have multiple problems accumulate. Such problems require determining what you can control and what you cannot. This chapter is designed to help you determine what you can manage and to guide you in dealing with the areas that you cannot manage. First you have to understand what happens with change.

Understanding Change

Recovery is more than a shift of emphasis. It is a series of internal movements that alter one's life. How does dramatic change occur? It helps to understand the nature of change itself. Scientists have long noted that some changes are transforming and others are not. By looking at how systems work, including family systems, political systems, molecular systems, mathematical systems, and even computer systems, we have concluded that two types of change exist. They are first order change and second order change.

First order change is most accurately described with the French aphorism, "The more things change, the more they stay the same." They are concrete actions taken to quickly stop a problem and to address specific consequences. Consider the woman who marries three abusive alcoholics in a row. Each one is worse than the last. Yet, before each marriage, she was determined to do better than before. The harder she tried, the worse the marriage and life became. Did she change? Yes, she changed husbands, but her situation remained the same. That is first order change.

Second order changes are those steps that people take to actually change the dynamics of their life and the way they live. The story of the woman above did not end with her three marriages. She began to look at her own life. She found a therapist and began going to Al-Anon. She learned that she had felt dependent on men and had few relationships with women. She learned that the criteria she used for selecting partners were rooted in beliefs formed during an abusive childhood and in intense feelings of inadequacy. She made new plans for herself, took a break from dating, learned to set appropriate boundaries, and eliminated the people from her life who abused her. That is second order change.

Addiction is a first order phenomenon. The harder addicts try to stop addictive behaviors by themselves, the worse things get. Those who abuse alcohol or drugs attempt to have their needs met through their addiction. The worst part is that this works for a while; they don't suffer consequences immediately. They can manage their alcohol or drug use and be fairly successful in their personal and work lives for awhile. This causes addicts to become grandiose in their thinking. They operate believing they can always pull it off. Yet, chaos begins to close in.

The painful reality of negative consequences teaches recovering people insights that lead to new "programming." First, they learn that there really are no secrets. They realize that they are unable (powerless) to change their behavior on their own; they need others. Finally, they begin to take a realistic look at themselves and discover the damage that has been done in every area of their lives and in the lives of their families and friends. Then comes a decision to put order back into their lives and to limit the damage. At this point, they begin therapy and join a Twelve Step or similar recovery program. The recovering person can either use willpower to try to make life different and stop the old behavior, or this same person can truly dig in and face the realities of life. In other words, recovering addicts can choose either first or second order change. Figure 5.1 will show you the difference between the two kinds of change and the requirements of each.

First Order of Change Addicts Believe:	Second Order of Change Recovering People Know:
• No one knows or will know the extent of my problems. • I can change behavior by myself. • I can always figure out or force a way to handle problems. • I work best alone. • No one is hurt by what I have done. • I have not been hurt by what I have done.	• There are no secrets. • I am powerless to change without the help of others. • Sometimes there are events that I can't control. • I need contact with others and their help. • Damage has rippled through the lives of people I know. • My behavior has disconnected me from myself.

Requirements of Each Kind of Change	
First Order of Change Addicts Believe:	Second Order of Change Recovering People Know:
• I must operate in secrecy. • I must isolate from others. • I cannot give anyone the whole story. • There's an easier, softer way. • I don't need others. • Chaos is the norm.	• I can be honest. • I must create support networks. • Trustworthy people get the whole story. • Integrity must become how I get my needs met with a lot less hassle. • I exercise humility and embrace mistakes and needs. • I have a damage control plan and seek the help of others.

Figure 5.1

Worksheet 5.1: **Your Turn**

Directions: List five examples of first order changes that you have made in your life in an effort to control your behavior or make your life different. Include such examples as changing jobs, moving, and leaving relationships.

1. _____

_____

2. _____

_____

3. _____

_____

4. _____

_____

5. _____

_____

What were some of the beliefs that led you to attempt to change your life by first order change only?

_____

_____

_____

_____

_____

_____

_____

_____

_____

Since you have begun this program, list five steps you have taken that have led to or will lead to true second order change. Don't forget the effort you have put into this workbook.

1. _____

_____

2. _____

_____

3. _____

_____

4. _____

_____

5. _____

_____

Provisional Beliefs

Stephen Covey, who wrote *The Seven Habits of Highly Effective People*, talked about radical change. He pointed out that, if you focus only on behavior, you will achieve only modest change. Significant change requires an internal "paradigm shift"—a change in the belief system that supports the addictive system. It includes all the personal perceptions that anchored the impaired thinking you learned about in chapter two. As in a computer system, you have to change the software to get a different result. You have to develop and install new programming. Even if you can think of examples of both kinds of change and differentiate clearly between them, you may not believe that true change is possible for you, or that you have any idea of how to do it. Until you do believe such change is possible for you, you will need to adopt provisional beliefs. These beliefs are an act of trust, held until your recovery process becomes stronger. Provisionally embracing the truths below will help you through the challenge that comes with starting change. They will help you as you begin to repair the damage caused by your addictive behaviors.

Critical Provisional Beliefs to Embrace in Recovery

- For the time being, you may not be able to trust your own perceptions. You will have to trust the perceptions of others, even as mistaken and unpleasant as you believe them to be.
- For the time being, you will have to trust that you have been damaged far more than you know, but that time and recovery can work wonders in repairing this damage and in helping you become the person you were meant to be.
- For the time being, you must remember that addiction is a form of insanity, in which you are deluded about reality. You need to believe that you must pursue reality at all costs. The only way out of this insanity is to tell those who are helping you all that has happened. They can support you in reclaiming reality. You must do this without minimizing or omitting awkward details. And you may not make private deals with yourself about holding things back. Anything less than full disclosure lowers the probability of your recovery.

- For the time being, you must allow people to care for you, even if you do not feel that you deserve anyone's love and care. You are important, valued, and appreciated in ways that are hard to accept right now. This means you must follow through on what is asked of you—to surrender control of your life to those who can care for you better than you can care for yourself at this time.

Damage Control Plan

Using these provisional beliefs, you are ready to create a new "order" in your life. You begin with a damage control plan. Most people at this point face problems and challenges as a result of their addictive behavior: arrests, loss of career, severe relationship complications, and disease, for example. The list may seem endless. Recovery teaches that it is important to get help and to keep things simple. Break all tasks into small component parts, and tackle them one at a time, and one day at a time.

Worksheet 5.2: **Current Problem List**

Directions: Use this worksheet to help you think through your damage control plan. Begin by making a list of the problems you are currently facing. You may wish to consult the problems list you made in chapter one. This list, however, should focus on your current problems that are caused by unmanageability, such as divorce, disease, unemployment, or an arrest.

1. _____

_____

_____

_____

_____

2. _____

_____

_____

_____

_____

3. _____

_____

_____

_____

_____

4. _____

_____

_____

_____

_____

5. _____

_____

_____

_____

_____

6. _____

_____

_____

_____

_____

7. _____

_____

_____

_____

_____

On the pages that follow you will find worksheets that allow you to think through each of the problems you just listed. Completing these worksheets will be helpful at the start of your recovery when things are chaotic and overwhelming. You also can use this process on an ongoing basis as normal life difficulties arise.

For each problem, you will be asked to write the following:

- **Best possible outcome:** What would be the best result of any actions you might take or you might devise?
- **Minimal acceptable outcome:** What is the minimal result that is acceptable?
- **Possible solutions:** Gather all the solutions that you and the people in your support suggest. List each one, no matter how far fetched it may seem.
- **Best solution:** From all possible solutions, combine or choose the ideas that might work best for you.
- **Action steps with target dates:** What concrete actions do you need to take? By what date will you take them?
- **Support needed:** What do you need in order to take these steps and who do you need to help you with this solution?

By carefully laying out your action steps and including the support you need, the tasks do not seem so overwhelming. You will have also met the requirements of second order change. This process will help you build support systems and deal with problems in ways that can help you throughout your recovery.

Worksheet 5.3: **Damage Control Plan #1**

Directions: This worksheet will help you look at the first problem you listed on Worksheet 5.2 (page 136) in an organized and logical way. Use one worksheet for each problem you listed. If you need more space (and many people do) simply continue the process in your journal.

Problem:

_____

_____

_____

_____

_____

_____

_____

Best Possible Outcome:

_____

_____

_____

_____

_____

_____

_____

Minimum Acceptable Outcome:

_____

_____

_____

_____

_____

_____

_____

_____

Possible Solutions:

1. _____

   _____

2. _____

   _____

3. _____

   _____

4. _____

   _____

5. _____

   _____

Facing Addiction: Starting Recovery from Alcohol and Drugs

6. _____

_____

7. _____

_____

8. _____

_____

9. _____

_____

10. _____

_____

Best Possible Solutions:

_____

_____

_____

_____

_____

_____

_____

Action Steps:

1. _____

   _____

   Date taken by: _____

2. _____

   _____

   Date taken by: _____

3. _____

   _____

   Date taken by: _____

4. _____

   _____

   Date taken by: _____

5. _____

   _____

   Date taken by: _____

Support Needed:

_____

_____

_____

_____

_____

_____

_____

_____

_____

_____

_____

_____

_____

_____

_____

_____

_____

_____

_____

_____

Worksheet 5.4: **Damage Control Plan #2**

Directions: This worksheet will help you look at the second problem you listed on Worksheet 5.2 (page 136) in an organized and logical way. Use one worksheet for each problem you listed. If you need more space (and many people do) simply continue the process in your journal.

Problem:

_____

_____

_____

_____

_____

_____

Best Possible Outcome:

_____

_____

_____

_____

_____

_____

_____

Minimum Acceptable Outcome:

_____

_____

_____

_____

_____

_____

_____

_____

Possible Solutions:

1. _____

   _____

2. _____

   _____

3. _____

   _____

4. _____

   _____

5. _____

   _____

6. _____

_____

7. _____

_____

8. _____

_____

9. _____

_____

10. _____

_____

Best Possible Solutions:

_____

_____

_____

_____

_____

_____

_____

_____

Action Steps:

1. _____

   _____

   Date taken by: _____

2. _____

   _____

   Date taken by: _____

3. _____

   _____

   Date taken by: _____

4. _____

   _____

   Date taken by: _____

5. _____

   _____

   Date taken by: _____

Support Needed:

_____

_____

_____

_____

_____

_____

_____

_____

_____

_____

_____

_____

_____

_____

_____

_____

_____

_____

_____

Worksheet 5.5: **Damage Control Plan #3**

Directions: This worksheet will help you look at the third problem you listed on Worksheet 5.2 (page 136) in an organized and logical way. Use one worksheet for each problem you listed. If you need more space (and many people do) simply continue the process in your journal.

Problem:

_____

_____

_____

_____

_____

_____

_____

_____

Best Possible Outcome:

_____

_____

_____

_____

_____

_____

_____

_____

Minimum Acceptable Outcome:

_____

_____

_____

_____

_____

_____

_____

Possible Solutions:

1. _____

   _____

2. _____

   _____

3. _____

   _____

4. _____

   _____

5. _____

   _____

6. _____

_____

7. _____

_____

8. _____

_____

9. _____

_____

10. _____

_____

Best Possible Solutions:

_____

_____

_____

_____

_____

_____

_____

Action Steps:

1. _____

   _____

   Date taken by: _____

2. _____

   _____

   Date taken by: _____

3. _____

   _____

   Date taken by: _____

4. _____

   _____

   Date taken by: _____

5. _____

   _____

   Date taken by: _____

Support Needed:

_____

_____

_____

_____

_____

_____

_____

_____

_____

_____

_____

_____

_____

_____

_____

_____

_____

_____

_____

_____

Worksheet 5.6: **Damage Control Plan #4**

Directions: This worksheet will help you look at the fourth problem you listed on Worksheet 5.2 (page 136) in an organized and logical way. Use one worksheet for each problem you listed. If you need more space (and many people do) simply continue the process in your journal.

Problem:

_____

_____

_____

_____

_____

_____

Best Possible Outcome:

_____

_____

_____

_____

_____

_____

Minimum Acceptable Outcome:

_____

_____

_____

_____

_____

_____

_____

_____

Possible Solutions:

1. _____

   _____

2. _____

   _____

3. _____

   _____

4. _____

   _____

5. _____

   _____

6. _____

   _____

7. _____

   _____

8. _____

   _____

9. _____

   _____

10. _____

    _____

Best Possible Solutions:

_____

_____

_____

_____

_____

_____

_____

_____

Action Steps:

1. _____

   _____

   Date taken by: _____

2. _____

   _____

   Date taken by: _____

3. _____

   _____

   Date taken by: _____

4. _____

   _____

   Date taken by: _____

5. _____

   _____

   Date taken by: _____

Support Needed:

_____

_____

_____

_____

_____

_____

_____

_____

_____

_____

_____

_____

_____

_____

_____

_____

_____

_____

_____

_____

Worksheet 5.7: **Damage Control Plan #5**

Directions: This worksheet will help you look at the fifth problem you listed on Worksheet 5.2 (page 136) in an organized and logical way. Use one worksheet for each problem you listed. If you need more space (and many people do) simply continue the process in your journal.

Problem:

_____

_____

_____

_____

_____

_____

_____

Best Possible Outcome:

_____

_____

_____

_____

_____

_____

_____

_____

Minimum Acceptable Outcome:

_____

_____

_____

_____

_____

_____

_____

Possible Solutions:

1. _____

   _____

2. _____

   _____

3. _____

   _____

4. _____

   _____

5. _____

   _____

6. _____

_____

7. _____

_____

8. _____

_____

9. _____

_____

10. _____

_____

Best Possible Solutions:

_____

_____

_____

_____

_____

_____

_____

Action Steps:

1. _____

_____

Date taken by: _____

2. _____

_____

Date taken by: _____

3. _____

_____

Date taken by: _____

4. _____

_____

Date taken by: _____

5. _____

_____

Date taken by: _____

Support Needed:

_____

_____

_____

_____

_____

_____

_____

_____

_____

_____

_____

_____

_____

_____

_____

_____

_____

_____

_____

_____

Worksheet 5.8: **Damage Control Plan #6**

Directions: This worksheet will help you look at the sixth problem you listed on Worksheet 5.2 (page 136) in an organized and logical way. Use one worksheet for each problem you listed. If you need more space (and many people do) simply continue the process in your journal.

Problem:

_____

_____

_____

_____

_____

_____

_____

Best Possible Outcome:

_____

_____

_____

_____

_____

_____

_____

Minimum Acceptable Outcome:

_____

_____

_____

_____

_____

_____

_____

_____

Possible Solutions:

1. _____

   _____

2. _____

   _____

3. _____

   _____

4. _____

   _____

5. _____

   _____

6. _____

_____

7. _____

_____

8. _____

_____

9. _____

_____

10. _____

_____

Best Possible Solutions:

_____

_____

_____

_____

_____

_____

_____

Action Steps:

1. _____

   _____

   Date taken by: _____

2. _____

   _____

   Date taken by: _____

3. _____

   _____

   Date taken by: _____

4. _____

   _____

   Date taken by: _____

5. _____

   _____

   Date taken by: _____

Support Needed:

_____

_____

_____

_____

_____

_____

_____

_____

_____

_____

_____

_____

_____

_____

_____

_____

_____

_____

_____

_____

Worksheet 5.9: **Damage Control Plan #7**

Directions: This worksheet will help you look at the seventh problem you listed on Worksheet 5.2 (page 136) in an organized and logical way. Use one worksheet for each problem you listed. If you need more space (and many people do) simply continue the process in your journal.

Problem:

_____

_____

_____

_____

_____

_____

_____

Best Possible Outcome:

_____

_____

_____

_____

_____

_____

_____

Minimum Acceptable Outcome:

_____

_____

_____

_____

_____

_____

_____

_____

Possible Solutions:

1. _____

   _____

2. _____

   _____

3. _____

   _____

4. _____

   _____

5. _____

   _____

6. _____

   _____

7. _____

   _____

8. _____

   _____

9. _____

   _____

10. _____

   _____

Best Possible Solutions:

_____

_____

_____

_____

_____

_____

_____

Action Steps:

1. _____

   _____

   Date taken by: _____

2. _____

   _____

   Date taken by: _____

3. _____

   _____

   Date taken by: _____

4. _____

   _____

   Date taken by: _____

5. _____

   _____

   Date taken by: _____

Support Needed:

_____

_____

_____

_____

_____

_____

_____

_____

_____

_____

_____

_____

_____

_____

_____

_____

_____

_____

_____

_____

Accountability and Honesty with Your Family

Alcoholics and drug addicts place their relationship with their addictive substance above their relationship with their family members. The alcohol or the drug becomes the addict's first love. They do not let their relationship with their families or friends get in the way of their addiction. They betray their families, lie, steal, and cheat. They do whatever it takes to keep from being separated from the alcohol or drugs. They let their families down over and over again. As a result, the families often feel confused, hurt, outraged, exhausted, or worried, and all trust is gone. Relationships become badly damaged.

Fortunately, these relationships usually can be healed when the addict takes responsibility for his or her behavior. The addict must be honest and accountable and show that he or she is trustworthy. The addict needs to acknowledge and apologize for past hurtful behavior. The Eighth Step says, "Made a list of all persons we had harmed, and became willing to make amends to them all." The Ninth Step says, "Made direct amends to such people wherever possible, except when to do so would injure them or others." These Steps are key to healing relationships with family and friends. When families see the addict showing genuine remorse and real honesty, they usually have enough hope to continue supporting the addict.

Accountability

When being accountable to your loved ones, you should address all of the key areas of life, including work, school, finances, health, and friendships. Most of all, you must address your relationship with family members. How did you damage these relationships in your addiction? What specific consequences exist in your life and relationships because of addiction? Typically, family members are desperate to see some honesty and accountability from you as an addict, and may help to repair some of the damage your addictive behavior has done to your relationship.

Worksheet 5.10: **Accountability**

Directions: In this worksheet, you will address how chemical dependency has impacted your life. Complete the worksheet, then with the help of a therapist, meet with your family members and review your answers. It can also be helpful to share your chemical use time line with them in conjunction with this exercise.

The following is a list of all of the substances I abused and am addicted to (or share time line):

_____

_____

_____

_____

My addiction has impacted work and/or school in the following ways:

_____

_____

_____

_____

My addiction has impacted me financially in the following ways:

_____

_____

_____

_____

My addiction has impacted my health in the following ways:

_____

_____

_____

_____

My addiction has impacted my friendships in the following ways:

_____

_____

_____

_____

My addiction has impacted my relationship with you,

_____ (fill in blank for each family member):

_____

_____

_____

_____

My addiction has impacted my relationship with you,

_____ (fill in blank for each family member):

_____

_____

_____

_____

_____

My addiction has impacted my relationship with you, _____

(fill in blank for each family member):

_____

_____

_____

_____

_____

My addiction has impacted my relationship with you,

_____ (fill in blank for each family member):

_____

_____

_____

_____

_____

    At the end of this exercise please describe to your family member your commitment to recovery and the strategies you plan to use to keep yourself sober.

Restoration of Trust

Addicts frequently ask, "How do I restore trust?" When they ask this question, they are often focused on a marriage or other primary relationship, although relationships with children, parents, siblings, and friends are also of great importance. First, let's look at what you should not do. Making fervent promises of not drinking or using drugs will not get you much at this point. Acknowledging how sorry you are is appropriate. Being defensive or blaming is like pouring gasoline on the fire. It works better to really understand how deeply you have hurt people. The goal is not to fill yourself with shame, but rather to develop resolve for change.

What makes a difference to people is what they see you do. *The only way to restore trust is reliable behavior over time.* Your family and friends won't trust you right away, and this makes sense. They must see you walk the walk of recovery, not just talk the talk. If your words match up with your actions, if you go where you say you are going, if you come home when you say you will come home, if your bank account reflects what you say about your spending, they will start to trust you. If you admit mistakes promptly and make amends, they will start to trust you. They will see the change as you go to meetings, work on your therapy, and make sacrifices to make recovery work. That is when they will start to trust. People start to trust addicts when the addicts start to trust themselves and when they act in a trustworthy manner. Those in your life intuitively know the process is working.

When partners and other family members realize they are hearing the truth, credibility begins to return. Here are some guidelines drawn from the experiences of many people who have gone through this process:

- **Give it a lot of time.** Most recovering people say patience is the most difficult, but also the most important, thing they learned. Phrases like *patience, go slow,* and *one day at a time* are useful. This reflects the old AA adage, nothing major the first year.
- **Be willing to lose it in order to get it.** In a primary relationship, both partners must resolve not to give up parts of themselves in order to keep the other from leaving. If you can be fully who you

are and your partner does not leave, you have something truly valuable. Fidelity to self is the ultimate act of faithfulness to the other.

- **Restore self first.** If you do the repair work that is necessary for your growth, your perceptions of your primary relationship will change dramatically. Most people's unhappiness in their relationship is about themselves, and not about their partners. You have to trust yourself before you can trust the other.

- **Accept the illness of addiction in the other.** Start by acknowledging at the deepest level of yourself that you and your family members are powerless and fully involved in the illness of alcoholism or addiction. This will be as difficult for family members as it will be for you.

- **Admit mistakes promptly.** Avoid blame. Work to be honest and accurate, not to prove who is right. Self-righteousness inevitably kills intimacy.

- **Share spirituality.** Explore ways to be spiritual with your partner and other family members. You have to find the meaning in your suffering, and doing so together can dramatically shift your perspective.

- **Make amends through Steps Eight and Nine of the Twelve Steps.** These steps are: *Made a list of all persons we had harmed, and became willing to make amends to them all. Made direct amends to such people wherever possible, except when to do so would injure them or others*. These Steps teach us to make amends by expressing regret for what we have done and doing what we can to make up for our mistakes. Use this approach as a model for daily living. Reverse the blame dynamic by taking responsibility for pain you have inflicted on the other. Do what you can to make up for it.

- **Remember, it is never going to be perfect.** Just as the ultimate partner, parent, or child does not exist, neither does the ultimate relationship. Accepting human limits in ourselves helps us be generous with our loved ones.

- **Socialize with other recovering people.** Include your family in activities with other families who are experiencing recovery. Attend open meetings with your partner. Go on couples' retreats and workshops. Support other families and socialize with them.

- **Have fun together.** All work (on recovery) with no play makes for great intensity, not intimacy. Closeness comes from shared common experiences—especially the fun ones. Remember, play is, in its own way, an act of trust.

The Trust Process

Addicts experience despair after getting drunk or high. And they promise themselves that they will never do it again. When they use again, they have not even kept the promise to themselves, let alone promises made to others. This repeated disappointment undermines the trust that addicts have for themselves. They simply are not doing what they intend. They can even tell themselves that this will have a bad end. And it does. Then they say, "I wish I would have listened to myself." Because we look at others with the same lens with which we view ourselves, addicts will believe no one else is trustworthy either.

Things start to change in recovery with damage control and honesty. Addicts take responsibility for personal behavior. In addition, addicts stop using and go through the pain of withdrawal. They stop relapsing. Once they have success doing those things, the shame dissipates. They start to trust themselves. Writer Robert Bly once remarked that growing up is making your body do what it does not want to do. Most addicts have not been able to develop normally, and so the normal maturation process starts. They start doing what they say they will, and they feel good about themselves. Up until this point, they have been filled with shame and have made decisions on the basis of what people will think of them. Now they are making decisions on the basis of what is right for them.

This is the turning point. Henri Nouwen, the theologian, described this process as the "conversion of loneliness to solitude." Addicts who spent years running from themselves now start to have a relationship with themselves. This means they have a compassion for themselves which results in self-care. Nouwen further points out that this ability to be true to oneself creates a new trust of others. They now can let others care for them. Once they trust others, they then start to trust a Higher Power. People who have trouble trusting a Higher Power often have significant trust issues. Nouwen says there are essentially three movements in a spiritual life, starting with trust of self, followed by trust of others, which transforms into a trust in God.

The Twelve Step program also mirrors that process. When addicts begin a recovery program, they admit how wounded they are. This is in the form of the First Step. By doing this, they also break the old rules of the addictive paradigm that says never admit how bad it is and never ask for help. As you will remember, this is part of the rule set that kept the addict in first order change. While sponsors and group mates cannot re-parent the addict, their care and constancy do accelerate the healing of the relationship deficits of the family of origin. The Second and Third Steps ask the recovering person to trust that a Higher Power will help them. For many, at first the group becomes the Higher Power. Eventually they start to "trust the process" and recognize there are larger forces at work in their recovery. This is how the second order change starts, which radically alters the rules that the addict lives by. The Second and Third Steps help the addict move from the provisional beliefs, with which we started the chapter to a new life based on a recovery paradigm.

This transition also lays the foundation for new relationships and real intimacy. As an addict, you may have partied with a lot of people, but the laughter and togetherness were not about who you were. In recovery the togetherness will be about sharing time and experiences with people who care for you. It will be about connecting with people on a deeper level so they know the real you. Intimacy is the connection of different people who know themselves and are true to themselves and, at the same time, honestly care about the other person. Healthy relationships extend from the self and require a level of trust and letting go that is very much in the spirit of Steps One, Two, and Three. Healthy relationships are a nurturing experience which can only happen when you allow people to know you and to care for you.

Use the Steps. They are a proven recipe for spiritual wholeness and successful recovery. Remember that the program started with the realization that without the spiritual component, recovery could not happen. Decide a spiritual life is essential, not an option. There are lots of resources for doing a Second and Third Step; some are listed on page 293 in the recommended reading list.

Suggestions for those who wish to cultivate a new spiritual life:

- **Find guides.** Listen to others share their spiritual experiences and ask how healing happened in their lives. Brokenness, failure, and tragedy have helped many people find parts of themselves they had not known. Many other people started their journeys with anger, fear, or skepticism, yet they found wholeness and contentment.
- **Separate religion from spirituality.** Many come with baggage about religious institutions that damaged or constricted their growth. Resentment about these experiences can cast shadows over genuine spiritual development. Organizations and institutions are not ends in themselves, but they can be utilized to help you have a spiritual life and build a spiritual community. Use only those which help.
- **Connect with nature.** Spirituality starts with a sense of marvel at our existence and the wonders of creation—other living things, oceans, mountains, forests, deserts, and changing seasons. Go for a walk. Watch stars. Take care of a pet. Notice your body. Play with children. Then connect these miracles with what else you see around you.
- **Make a daily effort.** The key to spiritual life is constancy. Daily rituals that anchor your sense of stability help you achieve incremental spiritual growth. Then, when leaps of faith are required and stress overwhelms you, a reservoir of accumulated strength awaits.
- **Find ways to promote reflection.** Spirituality is about what is meaningful to you and what gives your life value. Find strategies that help you to reflect on meaning and value. Make inspirational writing, daily meditation books, liturgy, prayer, journals, yoga and letter writing part of your daily rituals. These also help you make sense out of special spiritual events.
- **Surrender.** All inner journeys start with an "emptying" of self—a fact reflected in all religious traditions. Addicts begin recovery with an admission of powerlessness and live their lives according to the principle of "letting go." According to the Serenity Prayer, achieving personal peace involves doing all you can about an issue, then accepting that those efforts are enough.

Chapter Six: **What Is Sobriety?**
Managing Life without Alcohol and Drugs

"I will take the ring although I do not know the way."
—*Frodo, in J.R.R. Tolkien's* Lord of The Rings

In one of the beginning scenes of J.R.R. Tolkien's great epic, *Lord of the Rings*, the wizard Gandalf challenges the hobbit Frodo to bring peace to the land by returning the magic ring back to the land of Mordor. The return of the ring is the key to freedom from the tyranny of the evil magician Sauron. Gandalf holds out the ring for Frodo to accept the quest. Frodo feels a penetrating chill, which he immediately knows had been sent from Mordor to distract him from accepting the challenge. This evil sent by Sauron is designed to paralyze Frodo and render him incapable of responding to Gandalf. He musters all his courage and slowly raises his hand to accept the ring. He hears his own voice though it seems far away. He says to Gandalf, "I will take the ring although I do not know the way." Then begins Frodo's great quest that brings so much good to so many.

All the great stories of human courage start with the hero or the heroine not knowing how to meet a particular challenge, but starting anyway. So it is with recovery. In the Big Book of Alcoholics Anonymous, there is a famous phrase. "Some of us exclaimed, 'What an order! I can't go through with it.'" That is roughly akin to the cold chill from Mordor. It is the addiction trying to paralyze the addict from taking action. The people who succeed are the ones who move forward even though they do not know the way. Part of the benefits of the quest is what they learn as they do it. The point is they start by taking action.

Taking action means establishing sobriety. Another famous phrase from the Big Book is being willing to "go to any lengths" to get sobriety. Consider this story of a woman in the early days of recovery from an addiction to painkillers. She started on painkillers after back surgery. She had quite a few pills left over in her medicine cabinet after her back had healed. When she felt stressed, she took them and discovered that they helped soothe her emotional pain. Soon she was taking them all the time.

Ultimately, she started attending NA, got a sponsor, and stayed sober. She took care of an ailing mother, and eventually her mother moved in with her. She always went to two meetings a week, but she couldn't leave her mother, who had dementia, alone at night. She started skipping meetings, but soon realized she needed the meetings to keep her on track. She made a deal with a neighbor to baby sit her children one evening a week if her neighbor would watch her mother while she went to a meeting. This worked, but it was difficult. The woman was exhausted from working full-time and taking care of her mother; adding the neighbor's children to her caretaking load felt overwhelming. Still, she knew she needed the meeting so she hung in there. In the meantime, she started talking to other folks in the meeting about the problem and discovered that some of them needed care for children or elderly parents as she did. She worked on organizing a care center in another room of the church where they met. She asked meeting members if they would be willing to contribute to a caretaker's fee, she talked with the church about making an extra room available, she advertised for a caregiver, interviewed people, and after months she had established a care center where she could take her mother while she attended the meeting.

Today that group has grown enormously, attracting many others like her, who care for parents with dementia. It has also attracted many single parents. They have expanded the care center into two rooms and hired three caregivers. The meeting provides an invaluable resource for many people. It all started with one woman who wanted to maintain her recovery so badly that she found a way to attend meetings despite a tremendous barrier.

Sobriety rests on the internal decision that you will do what it takes to make your life different. It helps to understand sobriety as a boundary problem in order to make the decision work. Addicts typically have poor boundaries that result in poor impulse control. They learned in their families to take an easier and softer way. When the addiction took over, it became habitual.

The other part of the boundary problem is that they ended up doing things they did not intend or even want to do. Lack of boundaries also made them easily exploited by others. Many addicts come from abusive and dysfunctional families, which do not respect boundaries, so they do not have the judgment they need to make good decisions. The metaphor used to describe this point is a zipper. When you live in shame, the zipper to yourself is located on the outside. Anyone can unzip the zipper and gain access to your life in ways that make you feel used or belittled. For example, people with poor boundaries find it hard to say no to requests that make them uncomfortable. On the other hand, people with healthy boundaries have the zipper on the inside. They decide who gets access to their lives. They know where the line is between themselves and other people. Addicts suffer from boundary failure—especially in early recovery. For many, sobriety is the first concrete expression of meaningful boundaries. Having a clear statement about your abstinence allows you to start the journey back to being yourself.

"Having the zipper on the inside," staying with a plan, and doing what you said you would do are all part of developing good boundaries and reclaiming yourself. Poor boundaries, such as putting yourself in dangerous situations or exposing yourself to drugs and alcohol lead you to relapse. Developing good boundaries—learning to set limits—becomes a revolution in a recovering person's life. If you don't learn to set limits, you have no chance of staying sober. Your boundaries must be very rigorous in early recovery to sustain abstinence. Remember what we learned about addiction as a brain disease in Chapter Three. Your neurobiology is altered by addiction so that the part of the brain that exerts willpower is deactivated during a craving. The rational part of your brain has been hijacked by addiction and the consequences to your use will not be apparent to you. That's why your boundaries have to be set so firmly.

Most addicts have family-of-origin issues that underlie their poor boundaries, making it hard for them to set limits. These critical issues for being a healthy person include:

- achievement
- self-esteem
- self-care
- accountability
- realism
- conscience
- self-awareness
- relationships

In therapy, professionals routinely see recurring patterns for addicts in each of these areas that affect their ability to establish a relapse-free sobriety. Before exploring the basic elements of sobriety, you need to understand how these issues might undermine your efforts. While all these patterns might not be true for you, chances are some of them will fit.

Achievement. Two patterns of achievement stand out in addicts. One pattern can be seen in an accomplished person who works hard and is successful. These addicts are doctors, attorneys, executives, clergy, and entrepreneurs. They share a commitment to excellence and success that is so potent that they become very driven people. Minimally, they are constantly so stressed, they live in chaos and depletion. Maximally, they may have a problem with compulsive working. They never have time for family or friends; nor do they have time to reflect on why they are trying so hard. Their sense of worth is measured only by money, power, and recognition. They often are reacting to parents who were very successful, and they are trying to match that success. They may attempt to be better than others, seeking a "special kid" status, or even trying to settle some score. Whatever their motivation, their frenetic life usually is rooted in some crazy loyalty to the family that results in overextension.

They approach recovery as a "to do" list, opposed to a long-term process. Consider the addicted physician who spent the first three days of treatment using every spare moment to fill out the exercises in Dr. Patrick Carnes' book, *A Gentle Path through the Twelve Steps*. He even did a couple all-night efforts to complete the work. Of course, this is how he would study for medical school. He thought that, if he could fill in the blanks, he would have completed the work. He completed book and said he was ready to go home. It took him weeks to understand that he had relationships to build, decisions to make, and feelings to express. At the end of treatment, he laughed about how he had planned to make therapy a matter of filling in the blanks. If you are goal-oriented, it is a major accomplishment to understand that the process itself—how you get to the goal—is just as important as the goal.

The further trouble is that over-achieving addicts are used to living depleted and exhausted lives, which leads to entitlement and poor self-care. Addiction is fueled by deprivation. Overextension, chaos, and constant stress lead to depletion. Thus, when some type of career or material success is achieved, the addict starts to crave an inordinate reward. Their values, consequences, and reality all that go out the window. They say to themselves, "I worked hard, so now I deserve to get high." When an addict constantly achieves certain objectives, "I deserve it" becomes one of the anchors of the addictive system.

Underachievers are the flip side of this pattern. Often, they come from families that are very successful. Surrounded by success, the only way to succeed or even be noticed is to fail. These addicts become the family "problem." School, jobs, relationships, and responsibilities go badly. The addict feels lots of shame and a curious loyalty emerges. As long as the addict is the problem, no one has to notice the emptiness or the abuse in the family. So being a scapegoat serves a function. In recovery, addicts with this pattern realize that the family is actually invested in the addict staying in trouble. What would happen if they became very successful and happy? Who in the family would suffer? In other words, as long as the fingers are pointed at the addict, no else has to look at his or her behavior. Some even find their marriages have elements of the addict being "a problem child."

The further trouble here is that the pattern revolves around failure, problems, and disappointment. In all the chaos, pain, and despair, addicts feel they deserve some relief. They feel betrayed and victimized. That is often true because they have not taken care of themselves, making them vulnerable to exploitation by people who are both inside and outside of the family. The net effect is, "Things are so bad, I deserve to get high," or maybe, "So much has happened to me, I deserve to get high," or, "I feel so bad, I deserve to get high." The overachievers and the underachievers have the same result: they deserve it. In fact, some report having periods in life in which they combined both—when something bad happened, they deserved to use and when something good happened, they deserved to use. Finally, it reaches the point where something only has to happen and you feel you deserve it. The constant is convincing yourself you deserve it. Feeling that you deserve it is one of the surest roads to relapse. Sobriety will require you to look at how you respond to achievement and success, and where that fits in to your recovery.

Self-Esteem. Children should be made to feel special. Yet in some families specialness becomes problematic. A child can become favored over others, or be protected from or exempted from rules or tasks. The child can become what therapists call a "surrogate spouse," which means being a confidant or helper to the parent in things a spouse should do. The other parent may be absent, abusive, addicted, or deceased. The child becomes "the man of the house" or "daddy's girl." Because of this specialness, addicts may have been catered to, and, as a result, are not conscious of others. They can become very self-absorbed with meeting their own needs. They have a minimal sense of their impact on others. They place themselves consistently at the center of things. In its most extreme forms, we call this narcissism or narcissistic personality disorder. Remember, Narcissus was the Greek mythological figure who became obsessed with his own image. From a relapse perspective, it is difficult to maintain sobriety if you are not aware of your own limits or your impact on others.

The flip side is also true. Some children did not feel special. In fact, their self-esteem was eroded through abuse and neglect. Because they feel unworthy, they sabotage things when they could go well. They do not believe that they deserve success or attention. They are programmed for failure. Their attempts to do well are mined with self-fulfilling prophecies about not making it. We do become what we envision. If you do not believe that you can make sobriety work, it will elude you.

Either being self-absorbed or filled with shame causes the same result: a distorted picture of your place in the universe. For sobriety to occur, you must develop an appreciation for yourself that is not over-inflated or over-deflated. If you fit in either category, try this: take one hour and make three lists. Start with a list of events in your life in which you genuinely could take pride. Compare that with a list of times you programmed or "talked yourself" into failure. These are times when your own feelings of worthlessness kept you from doing what you needed. Also draw up a list of events when your preoccupation with self hurt those you care about. On the basis of these lists, make a quick list of your strengths and your limitations. You will eventually do this very thoroughly in the Fourth Step. Here, it is to provide perspective on what risks exist to your staying sober. You might wish to learn about using "affirmations." Essentially, affirmations help reprogram you so you can accept the lovable person you are. The path out of this is to find a way to affirm yourself from within so you have a realistic and confident sense of yourself. (See suggested readings on page 293.)

Accountability. Addicts typically resist being accountable. They resist being accountable because of how rigid or controlling their families were. Most feel that if they caved in to others' demands, they would lose their identity. That probably is an accurate perception, because in certain families, they would have a hard time developing a separate sense of themselves. Good parents accept the fact that kids do not want to do what their parents tell them, and they love them anyway. They are willing to work through conflicts and show kids the benefits of doing what you have to do. Part of being grown up is making your body do what it does not want to do. Kids learn the meaning of "no." They know their parents love them, and these parents are also accountable to their kids. For example, they admit their mistakes to their children. Children grow up knowing that it is OK to be imperfect, that it is important to be responsible, and that saying no is the first step in learning self-limitation.

Many addicts miss these core lessons. First, there are those who are never accountable. They do not do what they say they will. They do not admit their mistakes. They do not let anyone know what they really do with their time, their money, or their actions. Another category includes those who are accountable in appearance. In fact, many addicts are very disciplined publicly with reputations for hard work and integrity. Yet they have a secret life. They may have learned this is a way to escape the control and shaming ways of their family. Or maybe they learned it by watching the adults in their family. The net effect is that, on the outside, they are accountable, but if no one knows what they do, they are willing to do things that violate what they truly value. In business, the phrase is "keeping a separate set of books"—a false one for show, and a secret one for the vault.

Sobriety works only if there is total accountability. Your group, your therapist, and your sponsor become important links to accountability. A second set of books simply will not work. There have to be people in your life who know everything and who will challenge you.

Self-Care. Neglect is a common problem in the history of addicts. Busy or uncaring parents who do not take the time to help kids and show them how to live life really are neglecting their children. The children, in turn, fail to internalize skills in taking care of themselves. They do not do things to protect themselves from harm, and therefore are vulnerable to being exploited by others. They often see things they should do or prevent, and when disaster occurs, they kick themselves saying, "Why didn't I do something about that when I knew better?" They neglect their own bodies and welfare. In short, they do not love themselves enough to go the extra lengths for good self-care. For these people, sobriety is difficult because it requires a whole reorientation. They have to take care of themselves, or relapse will happen.

Other addicts lived with parents who did everything for them. They did not learn how to do things for themselves, expecting it to be done for them. We have seen this in wealthy families, in which "nanny kids" have every whim met—but still were not convinced of their parents' love. We have also seen parents of very modest means who protect and cater to kids, who, ironically, also feel unloved. The bottom line is grandiose entitlement. Everything is negotiable. No consequences really hit. No matter what the addict does, someone rescues him or her. They may even be outraged if no one does rescue them. They also are upset when things are not done for them. If they do not do what they need to do for themselves, they always say they tried. Recovery is a rude awakening here as well. No one can do your sobriety for you. Like Yoda says to Luke Skywalker in the movie, *The Empire Strikes Back*, "Do or not do, there is no try." Sobriety requires self-care. And you must do it for yourself.

Self-care means you do not put yourself in jeopardy. You do the regular things that maintain your health, including flossing when you brush your teeth. You consistently exercise. You avoid depletion. You let your friends do kind things for you. You figure out nice things to do for yourself. You take your recovery very seriously, let your sponsor help you, and go to meetings. Neither neglect nor entitlement works in sobriety.

Conscience. Some define conscience as the ability to follow the rules. To some degree that is true. Some addicts have no remorse for their behavior, even though they clearly hurt others. In its most extreme cases, we use the term *sociopath* when a person has no empathy for others. Drug addicts and alcoholics often hurt the people around them who they love the most. The addiction may be so powerful that it has taken precedence over your most important relationships. In recovery you will experience and express remorse for behavior that contributes harm to others. Recovery means taking responsibility for your behavior.

Part of the pain of addiction for many alcoholics and drug addicts is that they have violated their value system, and they are guilt-driven. One of the essential drivers of the addiction cycle is the despair after behavior you feel badly about. Addicts use more alcohol and drugs in an effort to blot out the despair. Torturing yourself for behavior that was exploitive or thoughtless adds power to the addictive process. The Twelve Steps help guide you through a process in which you do all you can to make amends and learn how to make peace with yourself.

Conscience involves more than following the rules. We call that compliance. A conscience determines that for which you will fight. If someone attacked someone you love, you would immediately put everything at risk to protect your loved one. A conscience asks what you are willing to put everything at risk for, because it matters so much. A person with a conscience comes to recognize that which matters. A recovering person draws a line in the sand, saying, "This is what matters to me. I will do everything for this."

Reality. People describe a person who is realistic and pragmatic as having "common sense." In short, people who have common sense learn from their mistakes. One of the most famous lines to come out of self-help literature is by author M. Scott Peck in his book, *The Road Less Traveled*, in which he writes, "Mental health is a commitment to reality at all costs." A frequently-quoted aphorism complements that statement: "Insanity is doing the same self-destructive behavior over and over, and expecting different results." Common sense is the ability to see what works and what does not. Learning from your mistakes is essential to your mental health.

We are not talking about delusion and denial here, although impaired thinking certainly affects this issue. We are referring to a deeper problem—that some people do not develop the ability to learn from mistakes. Usually, they come from families in which kids were not allowed to experience consequences. They never had to figure out that many of their problems were brought on by themselves. We do make our own happiness—and unhappiness. Some never learn common sense. Recovery, however, is built on common sense.

Others do have common sense, but choose to ignore it. This is the problem of willfulness.

Along with entitlement and grandiosity comes the addict's, "I want what I want, when I want it." To paraphrase a naval adage, "Damn the consequences, full speed ahead." Addicts are creative, resourceful people who shrewdly figure out how to overcome intrusive reality. Yet, sooner or later you have to learn from your mistakes and not rely on your damage-control skills. Recovery brings the additional reality of your addiction, which means you have to be realistic and accepting of your limits.

Self-Awareness. Typical addicts do not know much about themselves. In part, it is because of their beliefs around their own unworthiness. They feel so defective, they are uncomfortable being in their own presence. So they distract themselves with compulsive busyness, filling their lives with so much activity that there is no real interior life. They get uncomfortable with being alone, minimally having to have the TV on, or some other distraction. Many addicts have reflected that a fear of being alone was a significant factor in their behavior. Some addicts would either avoid or procrastinate on anything that would have meant delving into their feelings, motivations, and patterns. They even report mocking therapy and self-help. It simply was too painful. It was easier to dismiss any type of self-reflection as silly or useless.

Sobriety comes only with painful self-realization. Addiction is fundamentally a means to escape the internal turmoil. The core of therapy and Twelve Step work is to develop a functional relationship with yourself. It is the conversion of loneliness into solitude. In order for that to happen, you must use ways of reflecting on your recovery work. Readings, meditations, journaling, Step work—whatever you do, you must have sources of personal reflection built into your life. Further, there must be regular periods of down time to do the reflecting: rest, no activity, just being with yourself. These "windows of time" are incredibly important to your ability to sort out who you are.

Recovery groups use a phrase that author John Bradshaw popularized about becoming human beings, versus human "doings." Rest is necessary. Stephen Covey refers to it as one of the essentials of effective people. He calls it "sharpening the saw." One of the best books on this part of life is by Wayne Muller, called *Sabbath: Restoring the Sacred Rhythm of Rest*. Rest and reflection are key to an "examined" life.

Relationships. Addicts have incomplete relationships, at best. Most addicts struggle with isolation. They have to handle things on their own. No one knows how much they struggle. No way out of the shame exists for the addict who lets no one in. Ironically, many addicts are very social, but they hide the vulnerable parts of their lives. No one gets the whole picture. Along with accountability, one has to experience the acceptance and help of others in order to heal. It is the experience of other people that makes your self-acceptance work. One way to make sure sobriety is second-order change versus first-order change is to stay connected with people who know the whole story.

Affect. Therapists use the word "affect" to describe our emotional lives. Just as we need intellectual skills such as problem solving, we need emotional skills, such as handling anxiety and expressing our feelings. Addicts have "disordered affect," which means they do not handle their emotions well. People who are new to recovery often tell us that they struggle to have feelings. In many ways, they were punished for having feelings. In some families, it simply was not acceptable to have an emotional life. So to survive, your feeling life was shut down. It may have just been the family norm not to express feelings. Some people who are very smart learned to rely only on their ability to think and neglected the development of their feelings and intuitions. Perhaps the biggest reason is that life was just so painful, it was simply easier to numb everything. Numbing out is one of the benefits of addiction. It keeps the feelings at bay.

Others overreact. Simple things escalate into intense emotional drama. Addicts are particularly prone to using rage to manipulate and intimidate. This rage becomes a self-indulgent extension of "I deserve it" or "I want what I want when I want it!" Volatile, romantic, and intense relationships become a venue for emotional roller-coaster scripts of disappointment and excitement. The turmoil obscures the anxiety and the emotions underlying the dramatic scenes.

Whether high drama or numbness, the core feelings remain unacknowledged. Recovering people often have to start by labeling the most basic feelings of joy, pain, sadness, anger, and fear. That way they start to have clarity about what they are feeling. They learn basic strategies around anxiety, such as learning to stay in the here and now, as opposed to stirring themselves up by obsessing about the past or the future. The principles of letting go, summarized in the Serenity Prayer, become a life stance to deal with anxiety and control.

The Sobriety Challenges

People can have difficulty achieving sobriety, even when they have a relapse prevention plan, go to meetings, and work the program. Usually, their inability to stop using alcohol and drugs is rooted in one of the challenges to sobriety listed below. Figure 6.1 summarizes challenges to sobriety. Notice that each issue can fundamentally affect a person's ability to set limits and boundaries. You may have also noticed that you fit in more than one category, and that sometimes you fit both extremes within a category. That is normal for addicts. These are the most common issues. Addicts tend to come from dysfunctional families. As they grow up, they learn to cope in the extremes.

The Sobriety Challenges		
Underachieving despair	Distorted achievement	Overachieving depletion and chaos
Self-defeating shame	Compromised self-image	Self-absorbed obsession
Not accountable	Lack of accountability	Secret life
Profound self-neglect	Problematic self-care	Grandiose entitlement
No remorse	Impaired conscience	Guilt driven
No common sense	Faulty realism	Common sense ignored
Avoidance/ procrastination	Limited self-awareness	Compulsive busyness
Isolation	Incomplete relationships	Hidden parts of self
Shutdown feelings/ numbness	Disordered affect feelings	Indulgent rage, drama, intensity

Figure 6.1

All the plans in the world will not help if you do not see the underlying challenges. However, by clarifying those underlying issues and how they might limit your ability to establish boundaries in sobriety, you will be ready to define what sobriety is. That is our next task. Before starting, complete the sobriety challenges worksheet and discuss with your therapist and sponsor.

Worksheet 6.1: **Sobriety Challenges**

Directions: Listed below are each of the challenges addicts have to establishing sobriety. Within each challenge, there are extremes listed with a scale of one to five. One means not a problem, and five means a severe problem. Rate yourself in each category. In some categories, you may find yourself high on both extremes. Beneath each scale, record examples of your behaviors and specify how this behavior pattern might sabotage your sobriety process.

Distorted Achievement	
Underachieving Despair 1 5	Overachieving Depletion and Chaos 1 5
_____ _____ _____	_____ _____ _____

Compromised Self-Image	
Self-Defeating Shame 1 5	Self-Absorbed Obsession 1 5
_____ _____ _____	_____ _____ _____

Lack of Accountability	
Not Accountable 1 5	Secret Life 1 5
_____ _____ _____	_____ _____ _____

Problematic Self-Care

Profound Self-Neglect	Grandiose Entitlement
1 5	1 5

_____   _____

_____   _____

_____   _____

Impaired Conscience

Guilt Driven	No Remorse
1 5	1 5

_____   _____

_____   _____

_____   _____

Faulty Realism

No Common Sense	Common Sense Ignored
1 5	1 5

_____   _____

_____   _____

_____   _____

Limited Self-Awareness

Avoidance/Procrastination	Compulsive Busyness
1 5	1 5

_____   _____

_____   _____

_____   _____

Incomplete Relationships

Isolation
1 5

_____

_____

_____

Hide Parts of Self
1 5

_____

_____

_____

Disordered Affect Feelings

Shutdown Feelings/Numbness
1 5

_____

_____

_____

Indulgent Rage, Drama, Intensity
1 5

_____

_____

_____

Recovery Essentials

By working on your sobriety challenges, addicts notice that the very groundwork of their lives change. They start to see that they have spent so much time and energy on escaping from reality, from their own thoughts and feelings, that they do not really know themselves. Part of recovery will be discovering a self, allowing yourself to know what your feelings really are, knowing your vulnerabilities, and valuing the person you are, with all your fears and imperfections and needs. It will also mean recognizing and valuing your true strengths. For all the focus addicts put on themselves, they really do not know themselves well at all.

The proven recipe to deal with sobriety challenges is quite simple. Here is a summary of the recovery essentials.

- Reward yourself for good work.
- Affirm yourself.
- Be accountable.
- Take care of yourself.
- Know what matters.
- Learn from mistakes.
- Rest and reflect.
- Connect to those who know your story.
- Allow pain, joy, fear, and anger.
- Stay present.
- Engage in healthy relationships.
- Have boundaries with self and others.

Worksheet 6.2: **Reflections on the Recovery Essentials**

Directions: This worksheet will help you more clearly understand just what the "recovery essentials" can mean for you. Respond to the questions in the space provided.

Do only what is important. What important matters are being neglected in your life? What distractions from important priorities do you currently allow in your life?

_____

_____

_____

_____

_____

Reward yourself for good work. What have you done well lately that you have not yet rewarded yourself for? Why have you allowed this to happen?

_____

_____

_____

_____

_____

Affirm yourself. Write some affirming statements to yourself. Make the statements a genuine compliment for tasks you are doing well. How does it feel to do this? Why those feelings?

_____

_____

_____

_____

_____

Be accountable. In what ways have you been accountable recently? In what ways have you had lapses in accountability?

_____

_____

_____

_____

_____

Take care of yourself. What recent examples of self-care can you report? What recent opportunities for self-care have you missed?

_____

_____

_____

_____

_____

Know what matters. Have you recently gone out of your way or taken an unpopular stand because something mattered to you? Or, have there been times when you did not stand up for something important to you? Explain.

_____

_____

_____

_____

_____

Learn from mistakes. Are there certain mistakes you still make? Why?

_____

_____

_____

_____

_____

Rest and reflect. Do you have regular periods of rest in your life that you and others can count on? If not, why not?

_____

_____

_____

_____

_____

Connect to those who know your story. Who are the people in your life who truly know everything that is going on with you? When was the last time you were in touch with each of them?

_____

_____

_____

_____

_____

Allow yourself to feel pain, joy, fear, and anger. Have you avoided any feelings lately? Which ones? What was the occasion? Why did you avoid them? What can you do about this now?

_____

_____

_____

_____

_____

Stay present. Are there any recent occasions in which you missed what was currently happening because you were absorbed by thinking about the past or the future, or by preoccupation with work, stress, or daydreaming? What sense do you make of those moments now?

_____

_____

_____

_____

Engage in healthy relationships. Are you honest in your relationships? Have you been in an abusive or exploitative relationship lately?

_____

_____

_____

_____

_____

Have boundaries with self and others. Has there been a recent boundary collapse in your life? What did you learn as a result?

_____

_____

_____

_____

_____

Maintaining Your Sobriety

Karen started drinking in college. She had always felt socially awkward. She felt shy and self-conscious. She moved to a different state to attend college and didn't know anybody. When she went to parties, she found that alcohol made her relax and it was easier to talk with people. She liked the glow it gave her. One night after a party where she had been drinking a lot, she let a man she hardly knew take her home. He came in for a nightcap with her permission, and he raped her. She felt guilty, like it was her fault. She reasoned that if she hadn't been drinking she wouldn't have let him take her home, or she wouldn't have invited him in, or she could have stopped him. She was too ashamed to tell anyone. To soothe her shame, she started drinking more at home alone. Soon she was getting drunk every evening and waking up feeling sick.

Karen became engaged the year after college. Her fiancé confronted her about her drinking, and she went to treatment to please him before they were married. She did most of the right things: meetings, therapy, workshops and sponsor. Yet she left out parts—like the shame she felt about the rape. When memories came flooding back, she found herself craving a drink. When she got pregnant it was easy to stay away from alcohol; she was so excited and focused on the baby. But about a month after the baby was born she found the cravings coming back. She started skipping her AA meetings because she was so exhausted. She told herself she needed the time and rest more than she needed a meeting. She called her sponsor to talk, but she felt annoyed when her sponsor suggested she go to a meeting. My sponsor just doesn't get how hard it is to cope with a newborn, Karen told herself. So she quit calling her sponsor.

One afternoon an old drinking buddy stopped by to see the new baby, and she brought an expensive bottle of gin as a present. Karen took the bottle and thanked her; she didn't want her old friend to feel unappreciated, after all. As time wore on she thought more and more about that bottle stowed in the basement. She felt increasingly isolated as a stay-at-home mom. It was just too hard to stay in contact with friends. The afternoons before her husband got home were especially hard. It seemed like the baby was relentlessly fussy then. It was also the time of day when she was most tired and felt most stretched.

One particularly hard afternoon when her husband called to say he would be late, she went to the basement and dug out the bottle of gin. I need this to relax, she thought. One drink isn't going to hurt; in fact, it will help me because I really need something to help me relax right now. Soon she was having a drink to calm herself every afternoon. It wasn't long before her drinking was out of control and her husband would find her alone with the baby and drunk when he came home from work.

In another example, Curt's wife threatened to leave him when he would not quit using cocaine. He continued to use and even increased his use. After a year of threatening, she took their two children, moved into an apartment, and sued for sole custody. The judge awarded sole custody to Curt's wife with supervised visits for Curt, but she gave him a second chance. The judge told Curt if he went through treatment and stayed sober, he could increase his visits with the children to include overnights and weekends. Curt went through treatment and was sober for a year. The judge gradually increased his parenting time until he was caring for the children every other weekend. Soon he told his wife he wanted to have his children for an overnight during the week as well. She said that was never going to happen. Curt was very angry.

When his weekend came around, he had a wonderful time with the children. His wife picked up the children on Sunday evening, and he thought about the fact that it would be two weeks before he had them for an overnight again. He thought about his wife saying "no way" to him, and he felt more and more angry. Then he started to feel sorry for himself and wonder why he even tried. At that point he called an old friend with whom he had used cocaine. Curt thought he needed a diversion and he would just hang out with him. He went over to his friend's place. He did the same thing again in two weeks after his ex picked up the children. He felt so lonely. This time he went with his friend to a bar they used to frequent with old using buddies. I'll just have soda, he thought. His friend called him the following weekend when he didn't have the children and invited him to a party. Curt went to the party. Someone pulled out some cocaine, and Curt held the bag, dipped the spoon in, and pulled it out just to look at it. He wasn't going to use, just wanted to see what holding it felt like one more time. But once in his hand, it was irresistible. Oh well, he told himself, the judge would never find out if he did it just this once.

When Karen dropped her AA meetings it was the beginning of her relapse scenario. Curt's anger and self-pity were the beginning of his relapse scenario. It is imperative to have the total picture of your addictive cycle in order to maintain your sobriety. It is not enough to simply say, "I won't drink" or "I won't use." You have to map out carefully the most likely ways you will begin to use again and eliminate the roads that lead there. This process is called "relapse prevention planning." It starts with identifying the most likely scenarios of relapse. Start by describing the chain of events that go into your relapse.

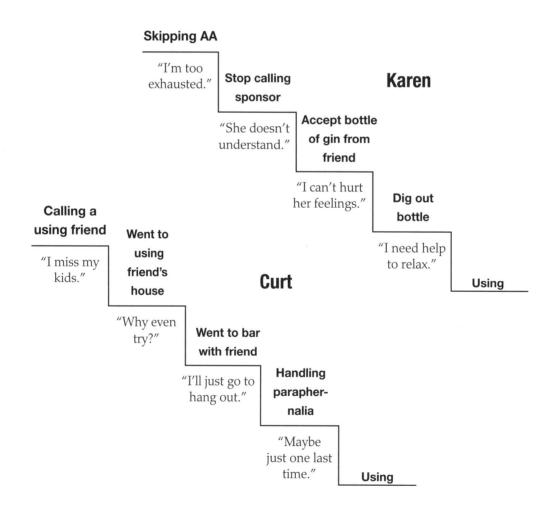

Figure 6.2

Relapse Scenarios

The following worksheets are designed to help you identify the most likely way you would start using again. If you are stuck, it might help you to review the work you did on your addictive cycles in Chapter 2 on page 55. Select the most probable ways you would set up using. In Figure 6.2 on page 206, the relapse scenarios for both Curt and Karen have been laid as if they were steps downward. Recorded on each step is a behavior, event, or action that leads toward using. Underneath each step is an example of Curt's or Karen's self-talk. These are phrases they would tell themselves to justify taking the next step. On the worksheets, map out and title each potential scenario you know could bring you to relapse. For example, Curt's might be "Calling a Using Friend." Karen's could be "Skipping AA." Also list the probable preconditions. Include such factors as depletion, anger at spouse, completion of project, or overwhelmed at work. Then return to the earlier section in this chapter on sobriety challenges. List whatever issues you have identified as potential problems within yourself that could contribute to this scenario. For example, entitlement, compulsive busyness, isolation, or ignoring common sense.

In the the lower left-hand corner of the worksheet, there is a place for you to list the probable outcomes. On the basis of your experience, what is most likely to happen because of these events? Further, you are asked to specify what the risks are. What is the worst that could have happened? When you have completed this analysis, share your work with your therapist, group, and sponsor. After you complete the worksheet, do the exercise on "fire drills." Then you will be ready to proceed to the next section in which you will write your sobriety statement. Use your journal or extra sheets of paper if necessary.

Worksheet 6.3: **Relapse Scenario #1**

Scenario: _____

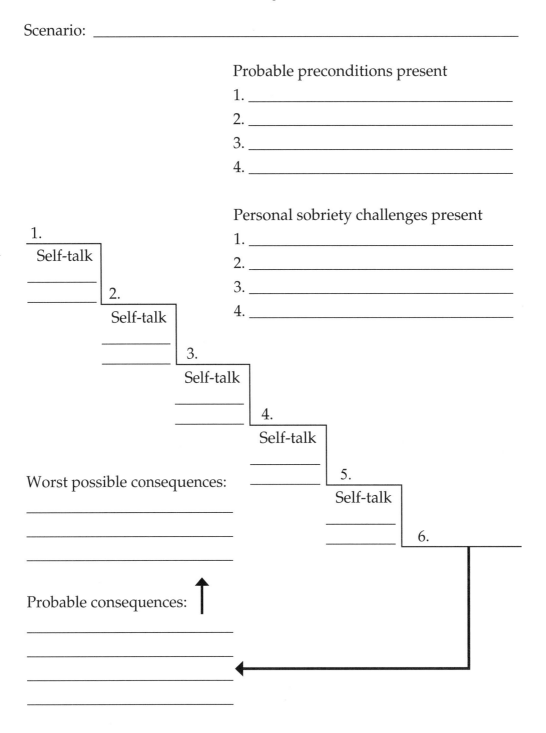

Probable preconditions present

1. _____
2. _____
3. _____
4. _____

Personal sobriety challenges present

1. _____
2. _____
3. _____
4. _____

1.
Self-talk
_____
_____

2.
Self-talk
_____
_____

3.
Self-talk
_____
_____

4.
Self-talk
_____
_____

5.
Self-talk
_____
_____

6.

Worst possible consequences:

_____
_____
_____

Probable consequences:

_____
_____
_____
_____

Worksheet 6.4: **Relapse Scenario #2**

Scenario: _____

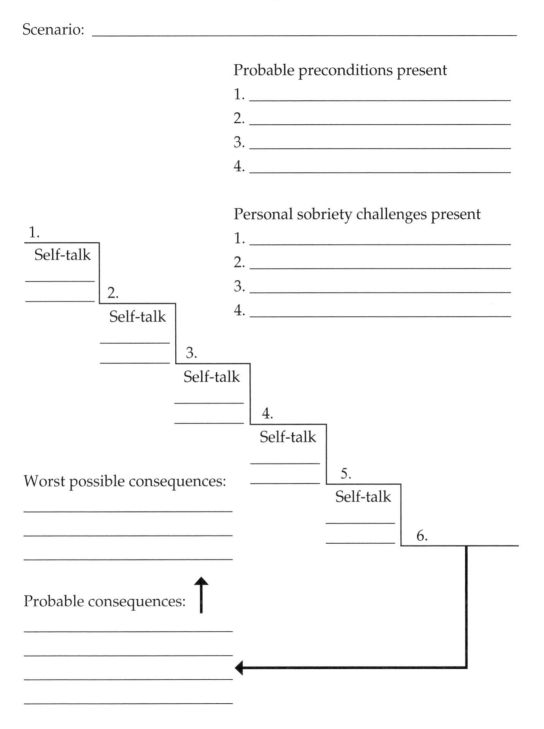

Probable preconditions present

1. _____
2. _____
3. _____
4. _____

Personal sobriety challenges present

1. _____
2. _____
3. _____
4. _____

1.
Self-talk

_____

_____

2.
Self-talk

_____

_____

3.
Self-talk

_____

_____

4.
Self-talk

_____

_____

5.
Self-talk

_____

_____

6.

Worst possible consequences:

_____

_____

_____

Probable consequences:

_____

_____

_____

_____

Worksheet 6.5: **Relapse Scenario #3**

Scenario: _____

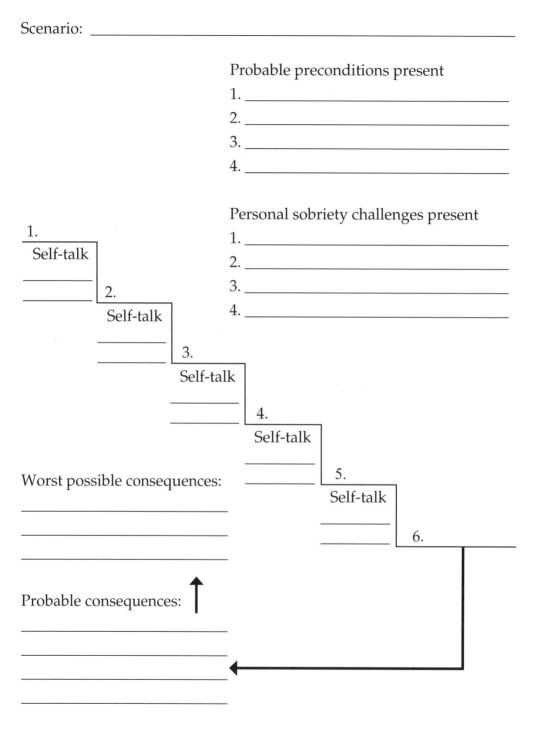

Probable preconditions present

1. _____
2. _____
3. _____
4. _____

Personal sobriety challenges present

1. _____
2. _____
3. _____
4. _____

1.
Self-talk
_____
_____

2.
Self-talk
_____
_____

3.
Self-talk
_____
_____

4.
Self-talk
_____
_____

5.
Self-talk
_____
_____

6.

Worst possible consequences:

_____

_____

_____

Probable consequences: ↑

_____

_____

_____

_____

Fire Drill Planning

A fire drill is an exercise in planning what to do in an emergency. In relapse prevention, a fire drill means planning what you will do if it looks as if you are about to relapse. To use the fire drill metaphor, you see and smell the smoke, and you know the fire is about to start. The fire drill is a routine set of steps put into action immediately, should trouble be near. This is an automatic protection plan. The success of the fire drill depends on three elements:

- a clear alarm (a good sign of trouble)
- very concrete steps to be taken
- a routine way to practice the concrete steps

Review the scenarios you have just completed. Complete the following exercise by listing symptoms or signs of trouble, specific action steps you can take, and ways you can practice (or drill) for resisting relapse. Show this worksheet to your group, sponsor, and therapist. Ask them to critique the steps you have listed. Encourage them to be honest, and be willing to listen. It could make a huge difference later. This extra effort on your part, along with the scenario worksheets, will help you to be thorough in making a plan to maintain your sobriety.

Worksheet 6.6: **Fire Drill Planning**

Directions: First, enter specific signs that there may be a relapse problem. Then, describe action steps you will take and indicate how you can practice the action steps. The success of the plan depends on how specific you can make it.

Symptom or Sign of Trouble	Practice or Drill Steps	Immediate Action Steps
Spending time with friends who use alcohol and drugs	*Call my sponsor regularly*	*Call my sponsor*
1.	1.	1.
2.	2.	2.
3.	3.	3.
4.	4.	4.
5.	5.	5.
6.	6.	6.
7.	7.	7.
8.	8.	8.
9.	9.	9.
10.	10.	10.

Healthy Recovery Plan

A healthy recovery plan has three components. First, there is the abstinence list. These are the behaviors that are part of your addiction. Part of your sobriety, then, is to abstain from these behaviors. Curt, for example, would write down using cocaine. Karen would write using alcohol on her abstinence list.

Second is the boundaries list. Here are the things you do not do because they create a hazard to your recovery. It is best if these are very concrete. Curt simply does not ever call a friend with whom he used cocaine in the past, no matter how lonesome he feels. He calls someone from his NA group or a new friend. If he does call an old using friend, that does not mean he has relapsed. But to do so does not add to his recovery. Karen might include in her boundaries list that she never misses her primary AA meeting. Later she may revise it to making sure she attends a substitute meeting if it is too hard to get to her primary AA meeting. A boundaries list might include being alone at night with extra cash in your pocket, or having lots of free time.

Finally, there is the healthy behaviors list that addresses what you are working toward spiritually, physically, and emotionally. It will address eight areas: friendship, family, romantic relationship, work/career, hobbies/interests, spirituality, exercise, and nutrition. Start by listing goals you have in each of these areas. Then list specific steps you can take in each area. Curt called an old using friend when he was feeling frustrated and lonely because he hadn't formed any new, healthy friendships. Curt might list "making healthy friends" as a goal under Friendship. He might write "ask Jim at my NA group if he would like to go out for coffee" as a specific step.

Taken together, these three lists become your healthy recovery plan. It is reviewed and discussed by your therapist, your group, and your sponsor. It becomes an agreed-upon contract about how you will conduct your life. It can change. For example, you may discover new behaviors that you need to add to the abstinence list or remove boundaries that are no longer necessary as you become healthier. Your healthy recovery plan will definitely expand as your recovery matures. Over the years, your healthy recovery plan (all three lists) will become a well-worn document that will serve you well.

Your sponsor or therapist may ask you to use the three-circle method of making these lists. To do so, take a large piece of paper and draw three concentric circles. The inner circle is the abstinence list, the middle circle is the boundaries list, and the outer circle is the healthy behaviors list. After completing each of the Worksheets 6.7–6.9, you will transfer that information onto Worksheet 6.10 on page 222 using the three-circle method.

If you need more space to write in than Worksheet 6.10 allows, you may use a larger sheet of paper and present it to your sponsor or therapist. Using a big piece of paper has the advantage of having all the information in one place, so it is easy to show to others. It is a very helpful way to do the work, affording a lot of space to work in. Other people can write comments and encouragement on it as well. You will find, on the following pages, worksheets to help you complete Worksheet 6.10.

Abstinence List

Abstinence means defining concrete behaviors that you will abstain from as part of your recovery. To use one of these behaviors again means a relapse. You identify these behaviors when you admit your powerlessness over them and you specify your unmanageability.

Boundaries List

Boundaries are self-imposed limits that promote health or safety. They may involve situations, circumstances, people, and behavior that you avoid because they are dangerous, jeopardize your abstinence, or do not add to your recovery or your spirituality. Boundaries are guides to help you toward health. Crossing over a boundary does not signify a relapse but, rather, a need to focus again on priorities.

Worksheet: 6.7: **Abstinence List**

Directions: List as many behaviors as you need to. Be specific and concrete. Remember that addicts often amend, add to, or delete from their lists as circumstances and recovery warrant. No change should be made, however, without consulting with your group, sponsor, or therapist. Once you have completed your abstinence list, transfer them to the inside circle on Worksheet 6.10.

Example: No smoking crack. No drinking alcohol.

Your Abstinence	**As of(date):**

1. _____

2. _____

3. _____

4. _____

5. _____

6. _____

7. _____

8. _____

9. _____

10. _____

11. _____

12. _____

13. _____

14. _____

15. _____

(Continue as required)

Worksheet 6.8: **Boundaries List**

Directions: List below boundaries that will help your recovery. Be as concrete as possible. Once you have completed your boundaries list, transfer them to the middle circle on Worksheet 6.10.

Example: Not going to happy hour with people I drank with, even just to drink a soda or coffee.

Your Boundaries	**As of (date):**

1. _____

2. _____

3. _____

4. _____

5. _____

6. _____

7. _____

8. _____

9. _____

10. _____

11. _____

12. _____

13. _____

14. _____

15. _____

(Continue as required)

Worksheet 6.9: **Healthy Behaviors Plan**

Directions: Start by listing goals you have in the eight areas of the healthy behavior plan (friendship, family, romantic relationship, work/career, hobbies/interests, spirituality, exercise, and nutrition). If you have difficulty—and most addicts do—get a consultation from your sponsor, group members, or therapist. After you have identified your goals, go back and list specific steps you can take and resources you might use. Remember, you are looking for areas you wish to improve. These are uncharted waters for many. Once you have completed your healthy behaviors plan, transfer them to the outer circle on Worksheet 6.10.

Example: *Romantic Relationship*

Goal: *I would like to be consistently honest with my partner.*

Action Steps: *Talk to partner about it. Practice open communications with my partner. Talk about feelings as they arise. Tell my partner when I am tempted to hide something. Make a list of reasons I disappear. Discuss in therapy.*

Resources: *Get help from partner. Ask therapist for strategies. Find books that can help. Go to workshop on honest communication. Do couples' exercises on communication. Talk to AA group about what other couples do.*

Goal: _____

_____

Action Steps: _____

_____

_____

Resources: _____

_____

_____

Goal: _____

_____

Action Steps: _____

_____

_____

Resources: _____

_____

_____

Goal: _____

_____

Action Steps: _____

_____

_____

Resources: _____

_____

_____

Goal: _____

_____

Action Steps: _____

_____

_____

Resources: _____

_____

_____

Goal: _____

_____

Action Steps: _____

_____

_____

Resources: _____

_____

_____

Goal: _____

_____

Action Steps: _____

_____

_____

Resources: _____

_____

_____

Goal: _____

_____

Action Steps: _____

_____

_____

Resources: _____

_____

_____

Goal: _____

_____

Action Steps: _____

_____

_____

Resources: _____

_____

_____

Goal: _____

_____

Action Steps: _____

_____

_____

Resources: _____

_____

_____

Goal: _____

_____

Action Steps: _____

_____

_____

Resources:_____

_____

Goal: _____

_____

Action Steps: _____

_____

_____

Resources:_____

_____

Worksheet 6.10: **Three-Circles Method**

Directions: After you have transferred the lists you created in Worksheets 6.7–6.9 (pages 215–221) in the template below, present it to your sponsor or therapist. You can also make your own three-circles on a larger sheet of paper if you need more room.

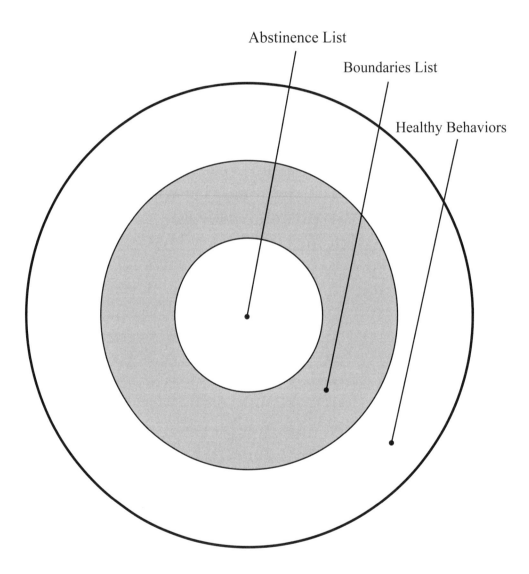

Abstinence List

Boundaries List

Healthy Behaviors

Preventing Relapse

Imagine a boulder on top of a hill. You have been given the job of keeping that boulder there. If it rolls down the hill, it will cause all kinds of damage. At the bottom of the hill is a large lake. If the boulder hits the water, it will be much more difficult to retrieve. The boulder serves as an important stabilizer for all that is around it, so it is important keep it up there. And if it were to fall, it is your job to return it.

As this big rock rests there, it takes little or no effort on your part to keep things in balance. But let us say that the land becomes unstable and the boulder starts to roll down the hill. Where is the best place for you to intervene? At the top, it might take only 20 percent of your strength to stop the boulder's momentum. By the time it is halfway down the hill, it might take 100 percent of your ability to stop it. At the bottom of the hill, it may have so much speed, you may not be able to stop it. Figure 6.3 on page 224 illustrates the principle of the boulder gaining momentum.

Obviously, it is best to keep the rock stable in the first place. But if you have to intervene, it is far better to do it at the top of the hill, than to try "last ditch" efforts at the bottom. So it is with recovery. It is better to keep stable or intervene early. Using the rolling-boulder analogy, let us construct how the addictive cycle can reassert itself in your life. A very predictable sequence of events occurs in relapse. These events follow the basic components you already know: obsession and preoccupation, ritualization, alcohol or drug use, and despair. By following the cycle, we can create an anatomy of relapse.

Obsession and Preoccupation—Relapse typically starts with lifestyle imbalance. Stress and neglect take their toll. Sobriety challenges start to appear. "I deserve it," "I want what I want, when I want it," and "Damn the consequences, full speed ahead," become the refrains. Urges and cravings appear, feeding obsession and preoccupation. The addict starts to distort reality and impaired thinking creeps in. Denial and delusion become partners with the obsession.

Ritualization—Boundaries start to collapse when addicts start to test themselves: Hanging out in neighborhoods where you got high. Window shopping in a drug paraphernalia shop. Calling a friend who is still using

Relapse Prevention: Loss of Control

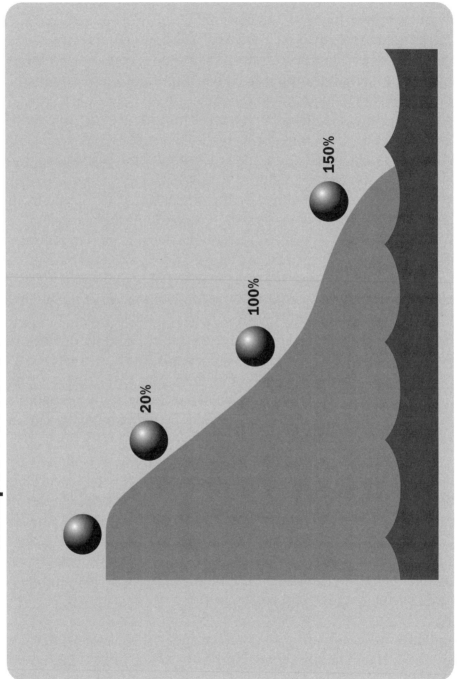

20%

100%

150%

Figure 6.3

just to say hi. These tests are really at the edge of the old ritualized patterns. Typically, active addicts do not have coping strategies in place to stop ritualized behavior.

Alcohol or Drug Use—Once there is an initial relapse addicts tend to say, "I have gone this far, I might as well do the whole thing." A famous pioneer in relapse prevention, G. Alan Marlatt, Ph.D., called this the "abstinence violation effect." In addictive thinking, the situation is now hopeless, which leads to ongoing use.

Worksheet 6.11: **Resisting Addictive Cravings**

Directions: Here are some strategies to help you resist addictive cravings. On a scale of 1 (poor) to 5 (strong), rate how effectively you use each of these strategies. Then write actions to improve your use of each strategy.

1. Develop spiritual strategies. Meditation, yoga, prayer—whatever strategies help you connect with yourself and the rhythm of the universe—need to be deepened, strengthened, and practiced. Number one on almost everyone's list is the development of a spiritual base, a calm center, which helps you resist turmoil on the periphery.

Rating:　1　2　3　4　5

Actions I can take for improvement:＿＿＿＿＿＿＿＿＿＿＿＿＿＿

＿＿＿＿＿＿＿＿＿＿＿＿＿＿＿＿＿＿＿＿＿＿＿＿＿＿＿＿＿

＿＿＿＿＿＿＿＿＿＿＿＿＿＿＿＿＿＿＿＿＿＿＿＿＿＿＿＿＿

2. Decode feelings. Behaviors that are associated with your addiction are usually accompanied by feelings of shame, loneliness, fear, pain, or anger. Always check for these feelings. Remember that to escape a feeling by using does not resolve the feeling. If you cannot decode your feelings, consult with a sponsor, a therapist, or group members.

Rating:　1　2　3　4　5

Actions I can take for improvement:＿＿＿＿＿＿＿＿＿＿＿＿＿＿

＿＿＿＿＿＿＿＿＿＿＿＿＿＿＿＿＿＿＿＿＿＿＿＿＿＿＿＿＿

＿＿＿＿＿＿＿＿＿＿＿＿＿＿＿＿＿＿＿＿＿＿＿＿＿＿＿＿＿

3. Avoid trigger situations. Identify situations, persons, and circumstances that can trigger addictive responses. Respect your powerlessness and avoid those triggers. Remember, when in doubt, don't.

Rating:　1　2　3　4　5

Actions I can take for improvement:_____

_____

_____

4. Don't let negative self-talk run rampant. Your shame will cause you to beat up on yourself, which will make you even more vulnerable. Affirm yourself. Check out negative thoughts with other people. If you're struggling with toxic shame, talk about it with your therapist.

Rating:　1　2　3　4　5

Actions I can take for improvement:_____

_____

_____

5. Work on nurturing yourself. Exercise. Walk. Eat well. Rest. Enjoy massages, baths, and safe indulgences. Seek out nature, music, art, humor, and the companionship of good friends. Find time to take care of yourself. Make your living space a cocoon for your transformation. Buy yourself a teddy bear. You deserve this treatment.

Rating:　1　2　3　4　5

Actions I can take for improvement:_____

_____

_____

6. Avoid keeping cravings secret. Keeping your cravings secret will add to their power. When you feel like using, go to the people you trust so you are not alone. In general, secrets are about shame, and shame always makes you more vulnerable. Secrets will separate you from others in recovery.

Rating:　1　2　3　4　5

Actions I can take for improvement:_____

_____

_____

7. Find alternative passions. Practice hobbies, sports, and activities you enjoy. Cultivate these parts of your life so compulsive patterns in working, obsessing, or acting out have to compete with activities and interests that are rewarding. Alternative passions become new arenas for growth.

Rating: 1   2   3   4   5

Actions I can take for improvement:_____

_____

_____

8. Acknowledge your choices. Avoid the feeling that you are a victim. You are powerless over your addiction, but you are in charge of your program of recovery and your lifestyle. In most areas you have choices, which can help you achieve the balance needed in your life. Be proactive instead of reactive, by acknowledging to yourself and to others what your choices are.

Rating: 1   2   3   4   5

Actions I can take for improvement:_____

_____

_____

The most important strategy is to create a Recovery Zone. The Recovery Zone is a lifestyle that creates parameters, and if you stay within those parameters, you will be safe. The trick is creating those parameters.

Figure 6.4 on page 230 uses our boulder analogy and the addictive cycle to graphically show the progression of a relapse. The more the cycle engages, the harder the relapse is to stop. The obvious place to start is to keep the boulder from starting to roll in the first place. You have to build up a barrier that keeps you from going down the classic "slippery slope." On the following pages, you will find some suggestions about how to build that barrier.

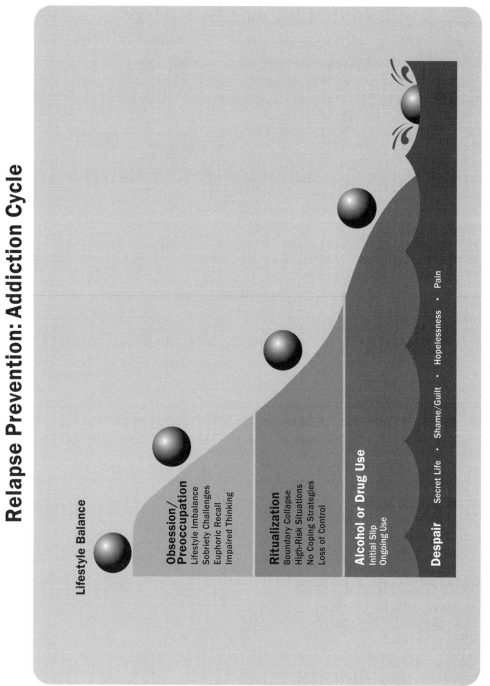

Relapse Prevention: Addiction Cycle

Lifestyle Balance

**Obsession/
Preoccupation**
Lifestyle Imbalance
Sobriety Challenges
Euphoric Recall
Impaired Thinking

Ritualization
Boundary Collapse
High-Risk Situations
No Coping Strategies
Loss of Control

Alcohol or Drug Use
Initial Slip
Ongoing Use

Despair · Secret Life · Shame/Guilt · Hopelessness · Pain

Figure 6.4

Creating Your Recovery Zone: The Personal Craziness Index

Most of us have had the experience of being really "on." Everything clicks together.

Complicated challenges seem effortless. Problems are simply problems, and you feel great. There is an optimum zone of psychological and physical health for each of us. An essential task in life is to figure out how to stay in that zone. Recovery, in many ways, is the reclaiming of that zone as you emerge from addictive illness. Sometimes recovery is perceived as an effort to avoid stress, when in fact, good recovery means *resilience*. We will always have stressors and challenges. Recovery is much like training for athletes. Olympic competitors or professional athletes know that, to succeed, they will experience great stress. Therefore, what they do is train for it. They work every day to prepare for the stressful event, be it a game or tournament. Similarly, recovering people prepare every day so that a stressor will not be overwhelming. They plan, they practice, they develop skills and strategies. They build their stamina and reserves so they can perform consistently. Sponsors and therapists offer coaching and mentoring so that when the challenge comes recovering people are prepared.

Some years ago, we developed a self-assessment process called the Personal Craziness Index or the PCI (pronounced "pick-key"). Over the years, it has helped many people establish basic parameters of their Recovery Zone. It starts with the basic practices that help us to be "on." Put another way, it keeps the boulder in place. When addicts actually observe and work their PCI process, it dramatically reduces the potential for relapse. To do it well takes time, and you may wish to refine it as you go. But the daily self-assessment of your PCI keeps you mindful of your Recovery Zone.

Personal Craziness Index

The Personal Craziness Index (PCI) is based on two assumptions: 1) craziness first manifests itself in a disruption of the routine, simple behaviors that support self-maintenance, and 2) behavioral signs will occur in patterns involving divergent sectors in our lives. Thus, we can be caught up in issues of cosmic importance and not notice that our checking account is overdrawn. If our checking account is overdrawn, we are probably out of socks also, because we have not done our laundry. If this pattern is pervasive, there is risk that our lives will become emotionally bankrupt as well—cosmic issues notwithstanding.

Addicts are particularly vulnerable to the "insanity" of loss of reality due to the neglect of basics. *Keep it simple* and *One day at a time* are guidelines borne by the experience of many recovering people. The PCI serves as a reminder each day of what we need to do. Without a process for such reminders, self-destructive behavior returns.

The process of creating your own PCI is designed to be as value-free as possible. Each person uses the index by setting his or her own criteria. In other words, generate behavioral signs (or as they are termed, "critical incidents"), that, through your own experience, you have learned to be danger signs or warnings that you are "losing it," "getting out of hand," or "burned out." The boulder is ready to roll. Thus, it will be by your own standards that you will prepare yourself.

Worksheet 6.12: **Personal Craziness Index**

Directions: The following are twelve areas of personal behavior suggested as sources of danger signs. Respond to each of the questions. You may substitute one of your own if you wish.

1. Physical Health. The ultimate insanity is to not take care of our bodies. Without our bodies we have nothing, yet we seem to have little time for physical conditioning. Examples are: being over a certain weight, having missed regular exercise for two days, smoking more cigarettes than normal, being exhausted from lack of sleep. How do you know that you are not taking care of your body? (List at least three examples.)

_____

_____

_____

_____

2. Transportation. How people get from place to place is often a statement about their lifestyles. Take, for example, a car owner who seldom comes to a full stop, routinely exceeds the speed limit, runs out of gas, does not check the oil, puts off needed repairs, has not cleaned the back seat out in three months, and averages three speeding tickets and ten parking tickets a year. Or the bus rider who always misses the bus, never has change, or forgets his or her briefcase on the bus. What are the transportation behaviors that indicate your life is getting out of control? (List at least three examples.)

_____

_____

_____

_____

3. Environment. To not have time to do your personal chores is a comment on the order of your life. Consider the home in which the plants go unwatered, fish are unfed, grocery supplies depleted, laundry not done or put away, cleaning neglected, dishes unwashed, etc. What are ways in which you neglect your home or living space? (List at least three examples.)

_____

_____

_____

_____

4. Work. Chaos at work is risky for recovery. Signs of chaotic behavior are phone calls not returned in twenty-four hours, chronic lateness for appointments, being behind in promised work, an unmanageable in-basket, and "too many irons in the fire." When your life is unmanageable at work, what are your behaviors? (List at least three examples.)

_____

_____

_____

_____

5. Interests. What are some positive interests, besides work, that give you perspective on the world? Music, reading, photography, fishing, or gardening are examples. What are you doing when you are not overextended? (List at least three examples.)

_____

_____

_____

_____

6. Social Life. Think of friends in your social network who constitute significant support for you and are not family or significant others. When you become isolated, alienated, or disconnected, what behaviors are typical of you? (List at least three examples.)

_____

_____

_____

_____

7. Family and Significant Others. When you are disconnected from those closest to you, what is your behavior like? Examples are acting silent, overtly hostile, passive-aggressive. (List at least three examples.)

_____

_____

_____

_____

8. Finances. We handle our financial resources much like our personal ones. Thus, when your checking account is unbalanced, or worse, overdrawn, or bills are overdue, or there is no cash in your pocket, or you are spending more than you earn, your financial overextension may parallel your emotional bankruptcy. List the signs that show when you are financially overextended. (List at least three examples.)

_____

_____

_____

_____

9. Spiritual Life and Personal Reflection. Spirituality can be diverse and include such methods as meditation, yoga, and prayer. Personal reflection includes keeping a personal journal, completing daily readings, and pursuing therapy. What are sources of routine personal reflection that are neglected when you are overextended? (List at least three examples.)

_____

_____

_____

_____

10. Other Addictions or Symptom Behaviors. Compulsive behaviors that have negative consequences are symptomatic of your general well-being or the state of your overall recovery. When you watch inordinate amounts of TV, overeat, bite your nails—any habit you feel bad about afterward—these can be signs of burnout or possible relapse. Symptom behaviors are evidence of overextension, such as forgetfulness, slips of the tongue, or jealousy. What negative addiction or symptom behaviors are present when you are on the edge? (List at least three examples.)

_____

_____

_____

_____

11. Twelve Step Practice. Living a Twelve Step way of life involves many practices. When done consistently, they can be key to staying in your Recovery Zone. Group attendance, Step work, sponsorship, service, and Twelve Step calls become the foundation of a good recovery. Which recovery activities do you neglect first when you are leaving your Recovery Zone? (List at least three examples.)

_____

_____

_____

_____

12. Healthy Relationships. Engaging in exploitative, abusive, or otherwise unhealthy relationships are signs that you are not well-grounded in your Recovery Zone. What are signs that a relationship you are in is becoming or already is unhealthy? Are you lying to the other person in the relationship? Or leaving out important pieces of the truth? Are you afraid to say what's on your mind? Are your boundaries still firm, or are you doing things someone else wants you to do even when it's not right for you? (List at least three examples.)

_____

_____

_____

_____

Recording Your PCI

The PCI is effective only when a careful record is maintained. Recording your daily progress in conjunction with regular journal-keeping will help you to stay focused on priorities that keep life manageable; work on program efforts a day at a time; expand your knowledge of personal patterns; and provide a warning in periods of vulnerability to self-destructive cycles or addictive relapse.

Worksheet 6.13: **Recording Your PCI**

Directions: From the thirty-six or more signs of personal craziness you recorded, write down the seven that are most critical for you. At the end of each day, review the list of seven key signs and count the ones you did that day. Give each behavior one point. Record your total for that day in the space provided on the Personal Craziness Chart. If you fail to record the number of points each day, that day receives an automatic score of seven. If you cannot even do your score, you are obviously out of balance. At the end of the week, total your seven daily scores and make an "X" on the PCI graph to reflect your score. Pause and reflect on where you are in your recovery. Chart your progress over a twelve-week period.

My seven key signs of personal craziness:

1. _____

2. _____

3. _____

4. _____

5. _____

6. _____

7. _____

Personal Craziness Chart

Day/Week	1	2	3	4	5	6	7	8	9	10	11	12
Sunday												
Monday												
Tuesday												
Wednesday												
Thursday												
Friday												
Saturday												
Weekly Total												

PCI Graph

Week	1	2	3	4	5	6	7	8	9	10	11	12
50 Very High Risk												
40 High Risk												
30 Medium Risk												
20 Stable Solidity												
10 Optimum Health												

Interpretation and Use of the PCI

The PCI is useful in early recovery as recovery habits are established. Also, the PCI becomes helpful during periods of stress and vulnerability. Many simply use it as a daily reminder of their progress. These users change the items as they progress in their recovery.

To use the PCI, select seven items from the "critical incidents" you have already listed. Then following the worksheet instructions, you can generate a weekly score ranging from 0 to 49. A guideline for understanding your score follows:

VERY HIGH RISK 40–49	Relapse probable. Usually pursuing self-destructive behavior; overzealous about one's special interests; blames others for failures; seldom produces on time; controversial in community; success vs. achievement-oriented.
HIGH RISK 30–39	Relapse potential. Living in extremes (overactive or inactive); relationships abbreviated; feels irresponsible and is; constantly has reasons for not following through; lives one way, talks another; works hard to catch up.
MEDIUM RISK 20–29	Vulnerable to relapse. Slipping; often rushed; can't get it all in; no emotional margin for crisis; vulnerable to slip into old patterns; typically lives as if he or she has inordinate influence over others and/or feels inadequate.
STABLE SOLIDITY 10–19	Resilient. Recognizes human limits; does not pretend to be more than he or she is; maintains most boundaries; well ordered; typically feels competent, feels supported, able to weather crisis.
OPTIMUM HEALTH 0–9	Very resilient. Knows limits; has clear priorities; congruent with values; rooted in diversity; supportive; has established a personal system; balanced, orderly, resolves crises quickly; capacity to sustain spontaneity; shows creative discipline.

Tools for Staying in the Zone

In the story of Ulysses, there were mythical figures called the sirens. They were female and partly human characters who sang captivating songs to lure mariners to crash their boats on the rocks. Sailors would have to plug their ears or tie each other to the masts of their ships so they would not founder in the sirens' traps. The Greek stories of the sirens' songs always depict the songs themselves as intensely compelling, filled with the promise of quenched desire. The lesson, however, was to never trust the sirens' song—no matter how promising or believable.

As an addict, you know the siren song of addiction. Addiction specialists use the term *euphoric recall*. In alcoholism, the alcoholic remembers the fun of the party but suppresses memories of the vomiting, the hangover, and the car accident. The methamphetamine addict remembers the excitement of feeling all-powerful and blots out the eventual crash and feelings of paranoia. Like the mariner following the sirens' song, the addict founders on the rocks following the illusion of addictive promise. One of the hardest lessons addicts learn is that they cannot trust their judgment about these matters. They must ignore, silence, or distance themselves from the song. It will always betray you.

So how do you do that? Boundaries. Pat Mellody, a leader in the addiction field, tells the story of how he learned about boundaries in childhood. He attended Catholic elementary school and was taught by some abusive nuns. He was troubled with how they treated people and their verbal abuse. His mother told him that it was about them and not about him. He simply had to notice what they did but refuse to let it affect him. Pat's mother gave him the core advice about how to create a psychological boundary and not be affected by what other people say or do. In other words, he learned to intentionally create a psychological distance. The same process applies to those people or situations that seduce you down the path of relapse. You will notice their presence, but you know the false promise. You simply do not respond.

What follows is a series of tools that will help you keep that distance.

A Letter to Yourself

Imagine you were your own sponsor writing a letter to yourself, just at the time you want to get high. What would you say? By writing the letter and carrying it with you, you have a significant resource to pull out at the last minute. Simply writing it creates the psychological distance you need. Take it to your group. Have sponsors and group members write notes on the letter itself. Then when you read it, you will have their support as well. It can help you keep your sobriety.

Instructions: Address the letter from you, to you. Include the following:

1. What are the probable circumstances under which it is being read?
2. What are the consequences if you ignore the letter?
3. What would you really need at the time of a relapse?
4. Give criteria for behavior that is very clear for yourself.
5. What is the hope if you don't use?
6. What is at stake if you do use—what is the plea you need to hear at this moment?

The model letter on page 244 will give you some ideas.

Dear Chris,

When you feel like picking up, pull out this letter. Chances are, if you are reading it, there is a thrill at the thought of getting high. Please read to the end because if the thought is about using, chances are you are seriously contemplating it. So please read on.

Each time you get high is the same. There is the thought. There is the anger, the loneliness, the feelings of entitlement. But remember, every time is the same; you will regret terribly what you now want to do.

- You will have to worry about legal consequences.
- You will have fear you will overdose.
- You will despair over your broken commitments.
- You will feel pain at the people you disappoint.
- You will have to tell lies to cover up—always there are lies.
- You will have suicidal feelings.
- You will place all your career success in jeopardy.
- You will never enjoy it—you are always disappointed.
- You will lose yourself for days thinking about God's punishment, even though you know that isn't true.

Right now your addict is seducing you with promises that won't work. So figure out what you need:

- Are you hungry or tired?
- Are you angry?
- Are you overextended?
- Are you needing some type of care?

Find whatever you need and get it. Do not do the one thing that will make all of the above worse. The question is, if everybody could see what you are about to do, would you still do it?

You are lovable and worthwhile. You deserve getting your needs met in a way that respects your wonderfulness. Imagine spirituality that is peaceful, graceful, vibrant, and growing—not what you are about now.

Please listen to yourself. You know that it won't happen for you if you pick up a drug or drink. Think of all the times in the past when you felt miserable after using and overwhelmed with regret. Do not kid yourself. Instead, love yourself enough to let the temptation pass—let go. Call someone.

Love,

Chris

Emergency First Aid Kit

Make yourself a psychological emergency first aid kit. It can be a bag, a "medicine pouch," an envelope, or even a box. Place in it things that provide your life with meaning. Suggestions include:

- symbols of recovery, including medallions, tokens, sponsor gifts, and other articles that remind you of significant moments in your recovery
- pictures and mementos of loved ones
- spiritual items
- copies of pages out of this book
- letters
- favorite affirmations, meditations, quotes
- phone numbers of peers and sponsors
- any items that represent personal meaning to you
- recordings of special music

Keep this kit in a place that is easy for you to get to. If you feel you are about to relapse or already have relapsed, pull out the kit to get support for what you need to do.

Worksheet 6.14: **Relapse Contract**

Directions: Use the following contract as a way to talk to people important to you (sponsor, therapist, clergy person) about what you will do if you relapse. Make a copy of the contract for that person, and keep a copy for yourself.

I, _____(your name), do agree that if I have a relapse in my sobriety, to do the following:

I will make my very best effort to limit what I have done.

I will call you and let you know what my situation is.

I will also do the following (fill in whatever you and your support person think should be the first steps): _____

_____

_____

_____

My sobriety date is:_____

Agreed to on this date: _____

Signed, _____

Resisting Relapse

Let's return to the experience of being "on," when everything you do seems to be exactly right. All performers—singers, speakers, actors, or athletes—have had such an experience. You intuitively know what to do with no thought. You just seem to be able to excel. This can happen in business or with hobbies. Even in simply exercising, times occur when your body performs above normal. Athletes will talk about playing "over their heads," meaning far above their normal capabilities. Authors experience moments when words just flow and ideas come seemingly from nowhere. Artists speak of ideas taking form easily, and business people refer to deals "coming together." There are days when you are simply unbeatable. We have called this the Recovery Zone.

Neuroscientists tell us that this does not occur accidentally. Typically, these situations are the result of three factors: vision, practice, and resilience. Whether it be a fighter pilot rehearsing combat scenarios, or an athlete using guided imagery for peak performance, there usually is a guiding vision. Being able to visualize a specific result and focusing on that image adds tremendously to bringing that thought into reality. A growing body of evidence shows that following a vision can affect corporate success in business, and even accelerate healing in our bodies. You have to have a picture of it. Unfortunately, from a recovery perspective, the reciprocal is also true. If you do not believe in recovery, let alone have a picture of how it looks, your chances decline for being relapse-free. Then the familiar cravings will occur, virtually guaranteeing the relapse process.

In addition to having a vision, there needs to be practice. When athletes are "in training," they prepare daily for a stressful event, such as a tournament, game, or marathon. Each day they build their strength, push themselves to improve their skills, and practice strategies for winning. When they prepare for the stress, they are, in essence, activating the vision. As they train, however, they are careful not to "over-train." They "cross train" so that the demands on one muscle set are not too much. They find regular patterns of rest. They take care of themselves, making sure they marshal their resources and give themselves real rewards. In short, they cultivate resilience. Resilience means they have reserves, so when they meet the inevitable stressors, they are not pushed beyond what they can do. Rather, the reverse occurs. They perform beyond even their own expectations.

The Greeks had a term for this process. They would describe someone who achieved being "on" as having *virtu´*—meaning excellence. During the Middle Ages, the word virtue picked up moral connotations. Originally, it was about preparing yourself intellectually, emotionally, and physically to be the best you could be. In this sense, we can look at recovery as the equivalent of creating virtu´—the cultivation of excellence. Often, people who have successful recoveries talk about how easy things have become and how they are doing things they never thought possible. Sobriety allowed them to have a new vision for their lives, and using recovery tools and principles every day created the practice and resilience necessary to meet the inevitable stressors. We call this living in the Recovery Zone. Think of a zone as a specific set of parameters or boundaries; by staying in the zone, you are optimizing your performance. Identify that area of life, including work, relationships, body, sex, and spirituality, in which you thrive. The goal, then, is to live within that area or zone.

Inevitably, you will have stress in your life. As we noted earlier, lifestyle imbalance is the beginning of relapse. The key to relapse prevention is to stay in your Recovery Zone. In part, you already have started to define your Recovery Zone through your three circles and your Personal Craziness Index. The remainder of this workbook is devoted to helping you get clarity about living in your Recovery Zone. To summarize how far we have come, look at Figure 6.5 on page 251 that illustrates the basic stance for resistance to relapse. Notice that the boulder now is nestled in a hollow supported by lifestyle balance. Addicts can live in a Recovery Zone and be "in training," doing more than they ever thought they could, and being all they can be. When they experience challenges, they have prepared themselves for that. So there is a barrier of resilience that keeps them from even starting down the slope of relapse.

If events happen that overwhelm the addict, and they do start down the slope, four barriers exist to prevent disaster.

Barrier One. Living the recovery essentials (to review these, go back to page 198) can immediately pull you back into the Recovery Zone. Your Personal Craziness Index provides concrete measures that you are at risk. Your three circles tell you what you are working for. You have the stabilizing experience of knowing what you want in your life and, as your recovery matures, you will experience fulfillment. Finally, what anchors all this is a sturdy, enduring decision to commit to recovery. Using the classic language of the Big Book of Alcoholics Anonymous, it is the willingness "to go to any lengths." Most recovering people know that moment when they said to themselves that they simply had to do whatever it took to make their lives different. That commitment is the cornerstone of the first barrier.

Barrier Two. If the stone does get past the initial barrier and a momentum toward relapse does start, we have barrier two. This barrier starts with reality checks. This means that recovering people check out questionable thinking and ideas with their support network. Therapists, sponsors, and other recovering people can quickly spot impaired thinking. If your old sobriety challenges, such as grandiosity or entitlement should reappear, they can remind you that you have been down this road before. Most importantly, your support network helps you remember that it is important to everyone that you maintain your sobriety. What you do matters to your group, friends, and family. Also, your boundary definitions serve as a very clear guide to staying out of trouble. By this time you have learned to reward yourself appropriately and have competing passions so that you are not operating out of deprivation. Rather than struggling with shame, your basic Step skills (developed in Chapters Four and Five) can help you with your sense of being worthwhile. You are not a bad or sinful person for having to struggle with this addiction. A path exists out of despair that would give momentum to the boulder.

Barrier Three. Further down the slope, you check in about boundary violations. The abstinence list becomes the guide to your behavior. It tells you what you have committed not to do. Moreover, you have the letter to yourself to help bring you back to reality. If you should have a boundary that failed, it does not mean that you have totally relapsed. Your fire drills should kick in, as if you were on automatic pilot. You have recovery rituals, such as your daily meditations and meetings, which serve as an alternative to your acting-out rituals. You have learned new coping strategies in dealing with stress. All the resources exist to stop the momentum here.

Barrier Four. If relapse does occur, it does not mean total immersion in the addiction. To begin with, there is a sobriety statement that is a map to where you need to be. Second, you have your first aid kit and all the resources of the Twelve Step process to bring you back. You have a contract with people who care about you. You signed it when you were relatively sane. Just follow the steps you agreed to take when you made the agreement. If none of this works, you now have people who truly know about your illness and can intervene on your behalf. By getting this far in this process, you can never really be in your addiction without knowing how to get back. In effect, you have now spoiled the addictive progression. You will find the delusional thoughts just do not work the way they used to. You know that the addiction is the false siren, and that you basically are avoiding yourself. You used to wonder if it was at all real. Now you know the unreality.

What remains to start recovery for yourself is to look at the deeper issues of cravings and what happens to your body. Situations or places or things that you associate strongly with using will activate pathways in your brain that produce cravings—cravings so strong that they can override your willpower. Knowing how this occurs can help you guard against it. That is the focus of the next chapter.

Relapse Prevention: Recovery Tools

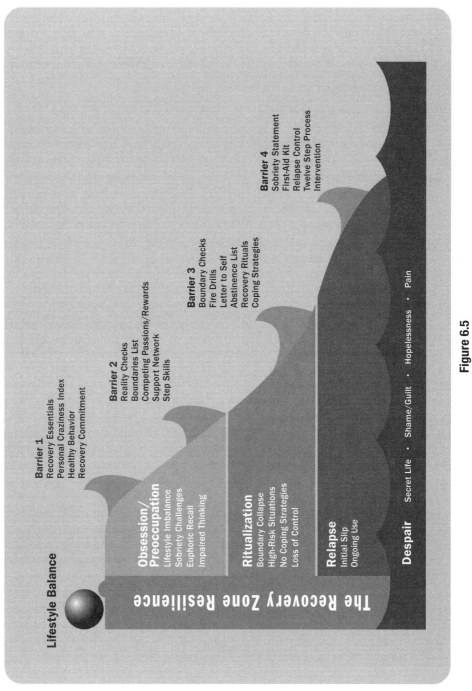

Figure 6.5

Chapter Seven: **What Has Happened to Your Body?**
How Expectations Affect Your Addiction

We tend to get what we expect.
—Norman Vincent Peale

Imagine two groups of wine drinkers. Each group is given identical bottles of wine. One group is told that each wine bottle cost ten dollars, and the other group is told that each bottle cost ninety dollars and is a rare vintage. The Stanford University researchers who did this experiment found that people who believed they were drinking a ninety dollar bottle of wine got more inebriated than those who believed they were drinking inexpensive wine. Basically, people's experience of getting high can be affected by their expectation of consuming what they believe to be the "good" stuff.

Addiction researchers have found this to be true across a wide variety of substances. What coffee drinkers believe about the type of coffee or caffeine in general will affect how impacted they feel. Cocaine users will react to cocaine in many ways based on what they believe it does for them. Even after a year of recovery, a cocaine addict will look at a picture of cocaine, and the brain will start to react as if cocaine was actually present. The bottom line is that not everything that triggers the pleasure centers is real. It is ironic that addicts seek out the "right" type of marijuana, whiskey, or tobacco, even though their brain creates a reality of its own as part of the disease. Once an addict's brain has been aroused by a substance, just the expectation of consuming that substance is enough to trigger the pleasure centers.

The brain gets tricked in the same way in other addictions. Problem gamblers all believe they have a method or some extraordinary way of pulling off a win, so they expect the pleasure of winning. Those beliefs are so strong that brain scans show even "near misses" are as exhilarating as actually winning. High risk investors—another form of gambling—believe so strongly in their ability to win against all odds that they distort reality. The result is one financial catastrophe right after the other. Bill W., the founder of Alcoholics Anonymous, was a big "deal chaser" in his drinking days. This is why he and his wife Lois ended up moving fifty-four times because of his money issues.

Sex addicts have such a strong expectation of pleasure from a sexualized behavior that the expectation alone triggers the pleasure centers. The behavior becomes so powerful that sex addicts will ignore obvious risks and put themselves in jeopardy. They have elaborate excuses for justifying their behavior, such as their spouse would not cooperate in doing a certain behavior, that they are too clever to be caught, or that their behavior is not serious. Sometimes they even think a specific person in the form of an affair partner, a stripper, or a prostitute is the person who will make all of life's problems go away. When reality comes crashing in they find that they have lost spouses and families, huge amounts of money, or have even been arrested and face jail time. What they believed as true (what we call the belief system), is part of the loss of reality.

All addicts have to examine their addictive expectations and beliefs. People who rely on substances or alcohol to cope have firm beliefs which help to activate their addictive coping. In fact, there is a logic embedded in their brain that is called a template. You may have used a template to draw a picture where you just follow the lines with your pen to create the same drawing over and over. Beliefs in the brain have been encoded in a biological path that repeatedly brings the addict to the same spot. Recovery requires that we examine the beliefs and the logic that cause us to act in certain ways.

Expectations Template

When completing the expectations template on page 255, if in doubt, ask your therapist, check with your group or sponsors, or ask a physician who knows about the affects of a particular chemical. Find out what the chemical is really doing to your brain and write it down. Writing it out will add reality so you can revise your beliefs and expectations. Recording your expectations template will reveal to you how your brain is sometimes "under the influence" of your beliefs as much as the chemicals you actually use.

Worksheet 7.1: **Expectations Template**

Directions: In column 1, list each specific chemical or substance you use. Include nicotine and caffeine. In column 2, write which type or brand is your preference. In column 3, write what you believe to be true about why you prefer this brand of wine, liquor, beer, drug, prescription, or chemical. Finally, in column 4, write your response to this question. What do you now know to be true about how the chemical really affects you?

If you need more worksheets, ask your therapist for additional copies or simply make your own. But be very thorough in this part of your work.

1 Substance	2 Preference	3 My expectations	4 The Truth is…

Changing Your Expectations Template

Your expectations of pleasure from a certain drug or alcohol is a well-worn pathway in your brain by now. It's not easy, but with practice you can change the pathway. It requires that you change your "self-talk." You will need to practice telling yourself the truth. Worksheet 7.2 on page 257 is a way to develop new "self-talk."

The Addictive Allies

All addictions tap into the same pleasure centers of the brain. This is why addictions work together. Consider the following:

- Michael was a day trader who made his living gambling with options and futures in the stock market. He felt that methamphetamines gave him an edge in his job.
- Sarah was a mother of three in an upper class very Christian family. She also was an alcoholic who had a significant secret sexual life. For example, she would look at pornography in the afternoon while her children and husband were gone. She always got drunk first. She felt ashamed about spending so much time looking at pornography, and she found that she needed alcohol to help her get rid of her inhibitions.
- Mark was a CEO of a huge company and he was known for his aggressiveness. Some of his critics thought him ruthless. He worked ninety hours a week and was relentless. He believed cocaine gave him clarity when he needed the extra edge. He bought the cocaine from escorts who he thought he deserved because they gave him "relief" from his stress.
- Shanna was obese. Her compulsive overeating was rooted in "comfort food." Marijuana was a way to escape while she binged on food.

Addictions are like partners that collaborate. Addictions have complementary beliefs that work together. Fill out Worksheet 7.3 Complementary Addictions on page 258, to see how different addictions are working in your life.

Worksheet 7.2: **Changing Your Expectations Template**

Directions: First, review your Expectations Template (Worksheet 7.1) and rate each substance and preference you listed by how powerful your expectations are. In the margin before the substance, write a 1, 2, or 3, with 1 being the most powerful expectation and 3 being the least. List all of the substances and preferences that you rated 1 in column 1. In column 2, identify how you usually got a specific type of substance for yourself. In columns 3 and 4, write what you will do differently or say differently to yourself to change that pathway.

1 Substance and Preference	2 How I Got It	3 New Behavior	4 Self-Talk
A certain kind of mushroom	I always flew to Amsterdam to get this mushroom.	I will not book any flights to Amsterdam.	That's a lot of money I can use for more important things.
Perrier-Jouet Champagne	I drove ten miles to Lakeside Liquor for this particular alcohol.	I will not take any route that goes by this store.	I can enjoy using that time for activities in my healthy recovery plan

Worksheet 7.3: **Complementary Addictions**

Directions: In columns 1 and 2, list your substances and the key beliefs you have held about them. In columns 3 and 4, list other addictions and compulsive behaviors that have supported your chemical use. Also note the beliefs you have held about these addictions and behaviors. Perhaps you required drugs or alcohol to indulge in certain sexual behaviors. Or perhaps you have used chemicals to help you handle your risk taking or your binge eating. See what patterns of beliefs emerge.

1 Substances I use	2 Beliefs about these substances	3 Addictions	4 Compulsive Behaviors

Putting It All Together

Over the course of your recovery your understanding will grow as you put together the pieces. A major portion of this work means digging out those beliefs that propelled you into all the chaos. If you listen to people who have been in successful recovery for a long time, you will hear them talk about discovering, even decades later, how the pieces fit together. You are beginning a process of reclaiming a reality.

Sometimes a picture is worth a thousand words. On the next page you will find space provided to draw a picture of all your addictions working together. It can be symbolic or it can be a scene or scenes out of your life. Allow your brain to come up with a snapshot of how the addictions were allies. On page 261, space is provided for you to summarize the dysfunctional beliefs and how you see them now as a sober person.

Summary of Beliefs

As we have seen in this chapter, addicts have many beliefs about their substances that simply are not true. Addicts also hold mistaken beliefs about themselves and about life that prompted them to use alcohol in the first place. For instance, an addict might have believed he was a worthless human being and no one could ever care about him, and he used alcohol to escape the painful feeling engendered by this belief. Or an addict might have believed she was a really boring person and no one would like her unless she was doing drugs.

Worksheet 7.4: **Draw Your Addiction**

Directions: Draw a picture of all your addictions and how they work together here. Remember that it does not matter if your drawing is artistic. What matters is that you create an image. The image is a new way of seeing connections between addictions.

Worksheet 7.5: **Summary of Beliefs**

Directions: Use this worksheet to look at all the beliefs that have gotten you in trouble. In column 1, list the beliefs that have driven your addictions. In column 2, write out what you feel and think about those beliefs now.

1 Beliefs that have driven my addiction	2 My current thoughts and feelings

Reclaim All the Ways You Have Lost Yourself

It is a common process for people to begin recovery by seeing how substances were taking over their decisions. However, it also common to realize as they progress that there were other addictive behaviors as well. If while doing this work you realize that you also need to face other addictions, you will be among the majority of recovering people. It is important to get help to address the other issues so that you reclaim all the ways you have lost yourself. Fortunately, there are many resources that now exist to help with this reality. The purpose of this book is to keep our focus on the chemical issues. But rest assured, stopping to get the larger picture helps immensely. Seldom do we have just one addiction at work.

Chapter Eight: **Where is Your Support?**
Creating Your Support System

*Practical experience shows that nothing will so much insure
immunity from drinking as intensive work with other alcoholics.
It works when other activities fail.*
—from *Alcoholic Anonymous*

Throughout this book we have identified the importance of being in a Twelve Step program. To summarize:

- At its most basic level, the recovery process requires connection and consultation with others. Addicts who are isolated make poor choices. To succeed in recovery, they need the help of therapists and of other recovering people. Starting with the initial debriefing with a sponsor and continuing through relapse prevention work, we have emphasized the importance of having recovering people involved in your work.
- The Twelve Steps teach an existential position that can help addicts better manage stress, grief, loss, and anxiety.
- Starting with the First Step, the Twelve Steps initiate a profound change process. The addictive system becomes altered beyond first-order changes in which the addict attempts to control behavior by "trying harder" to reduce consequences.
- Abuse victims and children raised in dysfunctional families find it difficult to engage in therapy unless they are with an ongoing group of people who have had similar experiences. Participating in a Twelve Step group helps addicts make up developmental deficits—that is, skills they did not get from their families—in such areas as intimacy, trust, and accountability.

In addition to being in a Twelve Step program, therapy makes a fundamental difference in how successful recovery is. Some addicts have been able to stay relapse-free with only therapeutic support, but those individuals who attend both therapy and Twelve-Step groups are more apt to be successful. Research shows that long-term recovery will consistently hold for those who immerse themselves into a Twelve Step culture. You have to start participating in the life of your Twelve Step community. How do you do that? This chapter will assist you in integrating Twelve Step recovery into your life.

Learning about the Twelve Step Process

To begin, it will help you to know more about the original Twelve Step group. We strongly suggest that you read *Alcoholics Anonymous*, the text known to recovering people as the Big Book. The recommended reading list at the end of this book cites a "study" version of the Big Book, which also contains a copy of the original typed manuscript. You will find this an extraordinary story of great courage and hope. Listed below are the original Twelve Steps of AA. By reading and reflecting on the original Twelve Step story, you will become familiar with phrases that have become the hallmarks of recovery, including phrases like "a day at a time," "an easier, softer way," and "cunning and baffling." You will find phrases that speak directly to you, whether you are addicted to alcohol, cocaine, heroine, methamphetamine, tranquilizers, marijuana, or any other drug or compulsive behavior. Moreover, you will become familiar with famous passages such as the "promises of AA" that have inspired generations of recovering people (see pages 83 and 84 of the Big Book). The Twelve Steps are listed below.

The Twelve Steps

Step One: We admitted we were powerless over alcohol—that our lives had become unmanageable.

Step Two: Came to believe that a Power greater than ourselves could restore us to sanity.

Step Three: Made a decision to turn our will and our lives over to the care of God *as we understood Him.*

Step Four: Made a searching and fearless moral inventory of ourselves.

Step Five: Admitted to God, to ourselves, and to another human being the exact nature of our wrongs.

Step Six: Were entirely ready to have God remove all these defects of character.

Step Seven: Humbly asked Him to remove our shortcomings.

Step Eight: Made a list of all persons we had harmed, and became willing to make amends to them all.

Step Nine: Made direct amends to such people wherever possible, except when to do so would injure them or others.

Step Ten: Continued to take personal inventory and when we were wrong promptly admitted it.

Step Eleven: Sought through prayer and meditation to improve our conscious contact with God as we understood Him, praying only for knowledge of His will for us and the power to carry that out.

Step Twelve: Having had a spiritual awakening as the result of these steps, we tried to carry this message to alcoholics, and to practice these principles in all our affairs.

Books describing the development of AA will also be useful to you. You will start to realize how truly revolutionary the Twelve Step process was and what it took for it to grow. Two books listed in the recommended reading are Nan Robertson's *Getting Better: Inside Alcoholics Anonymous* and Francis Hartigan's *Bill W.*

Two inclusive Twelve-Step Programs for those addicted to alcohol and drugs are Alcoholics Anonymous (AA) and Narcotics Anonymous (NA). AA had its beginnings in 1935. NA grew out of the AA Program in the early 1950s. In these programs, addicts gather in fellowship meetings at least weekly. The meetings take place in locations around the world.

There are also Twelve-Step fellowships to give support to family members and friends of addicts. These include Al-Anon/Alateen, ACOA (Adult Children of Alcoholics), CoDA (Co-Dependents Anonymous), and Families Anonymous. As in AA and NA, meetings can be found around the world. Since addicts so often have grown up in homes where a parent is addicted, many addicts report that they also benefit from attending fellowship meetings for families and friends.

The strong centralized Twelve Step support network for drug addicts and alcoholics has helped many addicts. There are central offices that provide easy access to information on meeting locations and publications. The listings summarize fellowship information and the additional reading section specifies key publications from various fellowships.

A.A. (Alcoholics Anonymous)

Mailing Address:
A.A. World Services, Inc.
P.O. Box 459
New York, NY 10163
212-870-3400 • www.aa.org

Location:
11th Floor,
475 Riverside Drive at West 120th St.
New York, NY 10115

N.A. (Narcotics Anonymous)

Narcotics Anonymous World Service
P.O. Box 9999
Van Nuys, CA 91409
818-773-9999 • www.na.org

Al-Anon/Alateen World Service Office

1600 Corporate Landing Parkway
Virginia Beach, VA 23454—5617
757-563-1600 • 888-425-2666 for world-wide meeting information
www.al-anon.alateen.org

Adult Children of Alcoholics World Service Organization

P.O. Box 3216
Torrance, CA 90510
562-595-7831
www.adultchildren.org

CoDA, Fellowship Services Office

P.O. Box 33577
Phoenix, AZ 85067-3577
888-444-2359
www.codependents.org

Families Anonymous

P.O. Box 3475
Culver City, CA 90231-3475
800-736-9805
www.familiesanonymous.org

The best action you can take is to find a good meeting, whether it is AA, NA, or another meeting. There may be thirty to fifty meetings in your city, but it may take some time to find a meeting that meets during the right time slot with people you like. That is, however, what makes the difference. More important than which fellowship you belong to is the quality of the meeting that you attend. Here are some signs to help you recognize a good meeting:

- Strong regular attendance is evident.
- Members take responsibility for leadership positions.
- Each week, someone in the group takes responsibility for presenting either a Step or a topic.
- The Step presentations or topic presentations are prepared and thoughtful.
- There is a well-understood and supported process for welcoming newcomers.
- The group has strong ties with a codependency or family support group such as Al-Anon, Co-Dependents Anonymous, Al-Ateen, or ACOA.

- There is a group life outside of the meeting in the form of regular meals together, workshops, or retreats.
- Periodically—at least every quarter—the group stops to do a "group conscience," which means the members hold an extended discussion about how the group is doing.
- Leadership and "jobs" in the group rotate regularly.
- There is a steady influx of new persons.
- There is steady attendance of veterans who have successful sobriety.

A good meeting is the heart of recovery. If you find one you really like, it is worth restructuring your schedule so you can attend regularly. It takes a while to know whether a given meeting is right for you. Many people suggest that you go to at least six meetings before you draw any conclusions. Every meeting can have an off night or two, but usually the character of the meeting will emerge over six weeks. Spend time outside the meeting over a meal or in some fellowship function getting to know some of the members. It would be unusual not to misjudge a meeting in some way early in the process. This happens, in part, because of the nature of meetings, but it also can be our own issues.

Early Barriers to Meetings

Addicts resist going to meetings because recovery principles are so different from the way addictions work. Meetings rely on their members to be open, consultative, vulnerable, accountable, and consistent. Addiction thrives best in secrecy, isolation, willfulness, and chaos. No wonder addicts find reasons not to go. The following are typical reasons people offer for not attending, as well as some observations about each:

I might meet someone I know.

You probably will, but that will help reduce feelings of shame for both of you. Reflect on the fact that while you were using, you ran the risk of meeting someone you would know and it did not stop you. Under which circumstances would you rather meet others you know? The real reason you do not want to go has to do with feelings of pride. You've tried to create an image of yourself that is different from who you really are. If someone recognizes you at a meeting, that person will know the truth about you. But this is exactly why you should attend. You will find that the pretense is unnecessary; people will respect you for who you really are, faults included.

I might meet someone I know professionally.

Physicians, therapists, attorneys, judges, politicians, CEOs, and business leaders worry about meeting clients, patients, or employees. This has been, of course, an issue in Twelve Step programs for years, one that people, particularly those in small towns, have successfully overcome. Several points should be remembered. First, this is a problem for everyone, and so this is where judicious use of boundaries applies. Being in the same program does not mean that you tell everything to people whom you know outside the program. Second, most cities have groups called boundary groups that are designed for people who would have a serious problem being in an open meeting. It would probably not be a good idea for a therapist to share struggles in the same group as his or her patients. Finally, it is very important to observe the traditions of the various fellowships and leave non-program issues at the door. It is not appropriate to talk to a CEO of a company about job possibilities at a meeting. Anonymity must be observed for the benefit of everyone.

I cannot find a meeting that does not conflict with my schedule.

If so, then start a new one. Get some help from existing meetings and your local intergroup, or call the national office of the fellowship of your choice. Tell local clergy and mental health professionals where and when you wish to start a meeting. Most meetings begin either because of a lack of meetings or the lack of meetings available at a convenient time. This task becomes harder, however, if you have never been in a meeting before. The fellowships have lots of experience in helping people start from scratch. So ask for help.

I do not fit well with the people in the meeting I went to.

The most common discovery mentioned by people who've joined Twelve Step programs is that they seriously misperceived the people in their group when they started. This happens most often because of the newcomer's shame, distrust, and uncertainty. Over time, they realize what tremendous resources the group members have become in their lives. You do have to get to know them, and the key to this task is spending time with them outside of a meeting. Frequently, groups meet before or after a meeting. In other cases, groups set up time during the week in which everyone gets together for a meal. Go to some of those events before you make up your mind about a group. This is one of the most important things you can do for your recovery besides finding a sponsor.

Everyone is relapsing in the group I go to.

If a pattern of relapsing occurs in your group, then it is time for a meeting called a group conscience. During that time, group members talk about how the group is doing and whether it is meeting the needs of its members. Members can share with one another how important mutual sobriety is. If people are struggling, they need to get more help until they are able to stay sober. Usually the group starts targeting topics that will help people with their sobriety. Sponsorship, regular check-ins by phone, and getting therapeutic support can also make a difference. Ironically, groups will often take the people who are struggling the most and give them more responsibility in the group, such as taking on the weekly trusted servant leadership role. Many people finally achieve sobriety when they are in a leadership position. Remember, some people may need a higher level of intervention, such as an outpatient or residential program, to give their recovery momentum. For them, simply being a leader may not be enough and they will need to be encouraged to get more help. Remember also the old aphorism, *You are only as healthy as your group*. Even as a newcomer, you have a responsibility to help the group be as healthy as possible. Not going to the meeting provides neither you nor the group with a solution. Sometimes, it is newcomers who provide the positive energy needed to make a group healthier. It is addictive thinking to say to yourself there is no hope because everyone is relapsing. Clearly, the real issue is to determine what you can do to make the group better.

I do not go to meetings because I have been relapsing, and it is hard to admit to my struggle.

Admit you are struggling. Start calling and meeting other people. Volunteer for leadership roles and fellowship tasks. Sign up to give talks and meetings. Start going to meals and get-togethers. Get more help if you need it. Above all, be honest with yourself about how you got outside of your Recovery Zone. The worst things you can do are to avoid meetings and to tell no one. These behaviors will start the boulder from Chapter Six rolling downhill. You simply must re-immerse yourself in the recovery culture.

Going to meetings is the bedrock of recovery. But attendance is not really the issue; involvement is. Do you have a sponsor who is coaching you? Even temporary sponsors make a huge difference. Do you participate in the life of the group? Have you presented a Step or a meeting? Have you supported the group by doing service work? Do you sponsor people? It is really "throwing ourselves into helping others" that makes the difference.

Consider the story of James. He was a successful man with a drinking problem. There were very few things he had set out to do that he had not achieved, but he failed repeatedly in his attempts to stop drinking. James was seeing a therapist, and he had found a Twelve Step group to attend. When he drank, James did not tell his therapist. He hated going to his Twelve Step meeting and acted like all was well when he was there. Admitting failure at something was still beyond what he could do. When his Twelve Step meeting finished, with most everyone adjourning to a nearby Chinese restaurant, James would head straight home.

James always felt wistful about missing the restaurant time because his meeting colleagues all laughed so hard and seemed to enjoy each other's company so much. He felt left out, and there were very few places in his life where he was not at the center of the action. As an excuse, James told himself that they did not have the stress he had, nor had most of them achieved what he had. He also told himself that his drinking had never been as bad as theirs. His story just wasn't as severe. And then, with time, James would allow the press of his schedule to interfere with his Twelve Step meetings. He would frequently cancel and reschedule therapy. As his recovery work became more erratic, James's drinking became more frequent.

James's life unraveled when he got into a serious car accident after he had been drinking. He was out of town and went to a bar where no one knew him. He thought he could pull off a drink or two and he didn't have to worry that someone would see him. However, a drink or two turned into five or six. Driving back to his hotel room, he hit a woman on a bicycle. She was initially in a coma and there was grave concern that she would suffer brain damage. Fortunately she made a full recovery, but not until after a long and difficult process.

James was criminally charged, put on probation, and ordered into treatment. The company where he was a vice president put him on a leave of absence. His wife had been threatening to leave him if he didn't quit drinking. He had managed to keep his drinking secret from her for the past year, but he couldn't hide this incident. She insisted on a separation. James had to move into an apartment and leave his wife and two children in the family home. He had to cash in part of his retirement account to meet expenses. In short, his life was a mess.

James went to see his therapist, Don, and reported what was going on. His drinking during the last year was news to the therapist—which he pointed out. Don asked James about his Twelve Step support, specifically who knew about the secret drinking. James could point to no one. Don told James that if they were to continue in therapy, he had to be honest about his use—and he insisted that James contact members of his group.

James called a group member named Jack that night. Jack said that he would invite some guys to meet together for breakfast the next morning. Three men met with James at a local pancake house. Coming up to the breakfast table, James felt teary realizing that these people whom he did not know well had changed their schedules to help him. Their welcome was warm and kind—though not without a touch of gallows humor. Laughing felt good to James, however. As he told his story in hushed tones, James fell again into tears first and then deep sobs. Here was the guy who would not let anyone know what was happening, crying in the middle of a pancake house. Being with men who cared about what happened to him broke down James' walls.

His group mates were very practical. They started with what needed to happen today. It was clarifying for James to realize that all he had to do was to get through today. Then they asked if he would talk to the group about his dishonesty with them. James agreed to do that the next night at the meeting. They stayed in touch with him until then. At the meeting, James admitted that he had been coming and saying things were fine when, in fact, they were not. Now he was facing the loss of career, marriage, and financial well-being.

When he finished his story, there was a long silence. And then people spoke slowly, thoughtfully. Some pointed out that they had done the same because it was the nature of the illness to hide shame. Others were relieved and glad that he was really finally joining the group. And still others offered their support and help. That night they all sat in the Chinese restaurant and helped James think through his next steps. They had suggestions for repairing his relationship with his employer, for therapy, and for dealing with an angry spouse. James came to two realizations sitting in that restaurant: his life had changed significantly because of these people, and he had seriously misjudged them. They were competent and resourceful, and their stories were no worse than his. Besides, they were working hard to keep him from making his life even worse.

James was asked by his company to go to a residential facility for treatment. When he went to see Don about it, his therapist said that he had come to the same conclusion. James had not been getting enough help, given how badly his illness had progressed. Don had also been talking with Judy, James's wife. In Don's opinion, to go into a treatment program was his best shot at recovery and saving his marriage. So James went. There, James was overwhelmed to discover just how much he did not know about himself. When he returned from treatment, he reported this to the group amidst cheers and laughter. He was elected to be the group's "trusted servant" for a three-month term. It was then that James really discovered the heart of the Twelve Step program. He became close to his sponsor (Jack took on the task), although he heard from almost everybody while he was in treatment. It had meant a lot to him to get supportive cards and calls. He now was sponsoring others and remembering them when times were difficult. He had discovered the secret to sustained recovery.

Service to others is how things get better. Back in the beginning of AA, Bill W. was told by Carl Jung that "passing it on" was how they would get better. The letters between Bill W. and Dr. Jung are now regarded as documents of great significance because of the recipe for success they contained. Addicts helping other addicts—"throwing ourselves into helping others," as Bill W. eventually described it—is a key to the Twelve Step program's success.

James' story is not unique. Many people who went through the motions of recovery were finally forced to surrender to the recovery process. Full disclosure to trusted people is one of those moments of surrender. Participating fully in a culture of Twelve Step support is another. In the following pages, you will find a series of exercises related to the "important" people in your life. The goal of the exercises is to ensure that you make a full disclosure to those in your life who need to know and whom you trust. Complete them and then record your reflections.

Worksheet 8.1: **Important People Inventory**

Directions: The following inventory asks you to list people who are important to you. You will categorize them in two ways. First, you will list people according to how much they know about you. Start with those who know everything. Then list those who know most of the story. Follow this with a list of those who know about your addiction, but not much of the story. Finish with another list of people whose relationship you value but who know nothing of your addiction or recovery. After completing the four lists, go back and rate each person on a scale of 1 to 5 as to how close you feel to that person. A score of 1 means not close at all, and a score of 5 represents a close and trusting relationship. Then, follow the directions provided at the conclusion of the exercise.

1. Important people who know the whole story (those who know everything past and present).

Name   Closeness Rating

a. _____   1 2 3 4 5

b. _____   1 2 3 4 5

c. _____   1 2 3 4 5

d. _____   1 2 3 4 5

e. _____   1 2 3 4 5

f. _____   1 2 3 4 5

g. _____   1 2 3 4 5

h. _____   1 2 3 4 5

i. _____   1 2 3 4 5

j. _____   1 2 3 4 5

2. Important people who know most of your story (those who know most everything past and current).

Name   Closeness Rating

a. _____   1 2 3 4 5

b. _____   1 2 3 4 5

c. _____   1 2 3 4 5

d. _____   1 2 3 4 5

e. _____   1 2 3 4 5

f. _____   1 2 3 4 5

g. _____   1 2 3 4 5

h. _____   1 2 3 4 5

i. _____   1 2 3 4 5

j. _____   1 2 3 4 5

3. Important people who know about your addiction, but have only few details (those who know of the illness, but do not know about the story, or recovery, or current progress).

Name   Closeness Rating

a. _____   1 2 3 4 5

b. _____   1 2 3 4 5

c. _____   1 2 3 4 5

d. _____   1 2 3 4 5

e. _____   1 2 3 4 5

f. _____ 1 2 3 4 5

g. _____ 1 2 3 4 5

h. _____ 1 2 3 4 5

i. _____ 1 2 3 4 5

j. _____ 1 2 3 4 5

4. Important people who know nothing of your addiction or recovery (those whose relationship you value but with whom you have shared nothing about your story or recovery).

Name   Closeness Rating

a. _____ 1 2 3 4 5

b. _____ 1 2 3 4 5

c. _____ 1 2 3 4 5

d. _____ 1 2 3 4 5

e. _____ 1 2 3 4 5

f. _____ 1 2 3 4 5

g. _____ 1 2 3 4 5

h. _____ 1 2 3 4 5

i. _____ 1 2 3 4 5

j. _____ 1 2 3 4 5

The following questions are designed to help you reflect on your Important People Inventory:

1. How do you feel about the number of people who truly know all of your past story and your current status?

_____

_____

_____

_____

_____

2. What discrepancies did you notice? Are there people you trust who do not know? People who know but with whom you do not feel close?

_____

_____

_____

_____

_____

3. Look at your inventory from a Twelve Step perspective. Who are the people in recovery on your list? Are there sponsors and sponsees? If not, why?

_____

_____

_____

_____

_____

_____

4. Who in your family is on that list? In your extended family? Do you wish to change that?

_____

_____

_____

_____

_____

5. Where is your therapist on this list? Do you need to talk to your therapist about your relationship? About further disclosure? About this list?

_____

_____

_____

_____

_____

6. This list often reveals unfinished business that needs to be addressed or relationship work that needs to be done. List any action steps you now need to take.

a. action step: _____

_____

b. action step: _____

_____

c. action step:_____

_____

d. action step: _____

_____

e. action step:_____

_____

Use this work when you reflect in your journal or talk to your groups. Show your work to your sponsor, therapist, or people in your consulting circle.

To Be of Service

To be of service means more than just helping in your group. Service may mean helping in your local intergroup, serving on a national committee, or going to a national conference. Service may also mean helping with some of the national support organizations. Join the National Council on Alcoholism and Drug Dependence (NCADD) which works to reduce the stigma attached to addiction and to make resources available to recovering people.

By now, it should be clear that working the program does not mean merely attending meetings. Nor is it just about sponsorship and doing Step work—although no change or growth will happen without those components. The real key is becoming an active proponent for the lives of those in recovery. Helping the organizations that support recovery is as important as helping after a meeting. Remember: helping others "takes us out of ourselves."

Chapter Nine: **What Makes for Long-Term Success?**
Deepening Recovery for Profound Life Change

"Do or not do. There is no 'try.'"
—*Yoda to Luke Skywalker in* The Empire Strikes Back

Film director George Lucas based his Star Wars Trilogy on the research of author Joseph Campbell. This story was created in part as a metaphor about meeting the challenges of twenty-first century life. At one point in the epic, young Luke Skywalker arrives on the planet Degobah in search of a master teacher of Jedi Knights named Yoda. Yoda, however, turns out to be very different from how Luke imagined he would be. He is green, short, big eared, and always placing his verbs in the wrong place when he speaks. Though clearly very funny, Yoda's humor nonetheless is always just beyond Luke's understanding. Yoda resembles what Native Americans call the "trickster"—the fun medicine man who teaches through paradox and practical jokes. Further, he always presses Luke to think beyond his world view and to question his assumptions. Luke soon learns that beneath Yoda's frumpish exterior and seemingly dim-witted manner is a learned, wise, powerful, and compassionate elder.

Above all, Luke learns from Yoda that being a Jedi Knight involves profound commitment. At one point, Yoda encourages Luke to attempt to raise his X-wing star fighter, which had sunk in a swamp. Luke makes progress but ultimately loses heart, thus allowing the ship to sink back into the goo. Luke tells Yoda that he "tried" to do as he was asked, but he concluded that raising the star fighter was impossible. Yoda responded by saying, "And that is why you fail!" Yoda then turns and raises the ship clear of the swamp and places it on dry land. Next, he turns to Luke and says, "Do or not do. There is no try." Then he walks away.

There is profound truth in that scene. Many addicts have failed because they did not believe it was possible for them to recover. They could acknowledge the possibility of others' success, but in their heart of hearts they believed they were too defective to succeed. But they always seem to want credit for trying.

These individuals failed because they never made the decision to change. They never believed in themselves enough to give recovery a chance. In fact, one of the most often asked questions among people in early recovery is, "Does it get better?" The answer is yes. Many addicts have lives that are much better. There are certain actions and thoughts that contribute to the success of people in recovery. People who have the greatest success take the same steps in a relatively predictable fashion. Sobriety is but one part of their life changes. They make a deeper commitment to making their lives better.

Here is the general profile of people who succeed in recovery:

1. They have a primary therapist. Whether they go to residential programs, intensive workshops, or take part in specialized therapy with others, they are involved with a therapist whom they stay with over a significant period. Working through a relationship with a therapist appears to be essential to recovery. Even more important, they each allow themselves to have an "examined" life in which one person (the therapist) knows them extraordinarily well and has skills to help them through the challenges they encounter as they move through recovery.

2. They are in a therapy group. Whether some of these hours are in a residential or outpatient setting seems to make little difference. Successful clients find they have spent time in group therapy, with someone who might or might not be their primary therapist, working on their chemical dependency. It is optimal to participate very regularly in group therapy.

3. They go regularly to Twelve Step meetings. Further, they become deeply involved in the program, including participation in service, sponsorship, and Step work. Working through all the Steps does make a critical difference; those who do not continue Step work either struggle in their sober life or lose their sobriety altogether. It is often recommended that addicts new to recovery attend ninety meetings in the first ninety days.

4. If other addictions are present, they are addressed as well. Addicts go to other Twelve Step meetings as appropriate for them. They come to understand how their addictions interact (negatively) with one another, and how they all relate to the deeper problems in their lives.

5. They work to find clarity and resolution in their family-of-origin and childhood issues. They use the Steps and therapy to understand the deeper character issues they faced, and they do everything they can to find serenity with them.

6. Their families were involved early in therapy. Early family involvement and support plays a significant role in recovery. Those who are able to resolve the conflicts and heal wounds in their families have reduced relapse rates. Oftentimes, the addict's recovery was the impetus for recovery and healing in other family members, too—though in some cases, years passed before this happened.

7. They develop a spiritual life. What their spiritual life consists of is as important as practicing it on a regular, even daily, basis. Those whose spiritual life flourishes are also usually active participants in a spiritual community.

8. They actively work to maintain regular exercise and good nutrition. People with solid recovery tend to exercise regularly, if not daily, and they are conscientious about making good food choices as part of their self-care.

Recovery Tasks

We have developed a model of thirty specific tasks that help people learn how to live consistent with this profile. These tasks are useful in recovery from chemical dependency. Table 9.1 contains an overview of the thirty recovery tasks.

You might think of these tasks like a food recipe: if you follow the recipe, you will have a positive result. You can, of course, add extra ingredients and enhance the recipe. But that's not necessary. In general, if you want good recovery results, follow this recipe.

Chemical Dependency Recovery Tasks

Tasks 1–7	Tasks 8–19	Tasks 19–30
1. Break through denial	8. Multiple addictions	19. Spiritual life
2. Understand addiction	9. Cycles of abuse	20. Resolve conflicts
3. Surrender	10. Reduce shame	21. Restore healthy behaviors
4. Limit damage	11. Grieve Losses	22. Family therapy
5. Establish sobriety	12. Closure to shame	23. Family relationships
6. Physical integrity	13. Relationship with self	24. Recovery commitment
7. Culture of support	14. Financial viability	25. Issues with children
	15. Meaningful work	26. Extended family
	16. Lifestyle balance	27. Differentiation
	17. Building support	28. Primary relationship
	18. Exercise and nutrition	29. Coupleship
	19. Spiritual life	30. Primary intimacy

Figure 9.1

Each task is finished by completing activities we call "performables." We have tried to define the performables as concretely as possible. By using the experience of others, we have created a road map to recovery. In other words, while you still may not know what challenges await you around the turns on your recovery road, you now know what has helped others succeed in recovery. Follow their lead and you will increase your chances of recovery enormously.

The First Seven Tasks

Research has shown that building a solid foundation for your recovery process is crucial. There are specific tasks that, if addicts do them, build strong recoveries. These first seven tasks are the backbone of your recovery.

The First Seven Tasks Performables Checklist

Directions: Listed below are each of the seven tasks you have accomplished. Under each is an additional list of performables—the specific activities you completed that make up each task. Review your work. Check off each performable if you wish. Notice how good it feels to "finish" what you set out to do.

1. Break through denial.

_____ Makes a problem list. (Worksheet 1.1, p. 12–15)
_____ Records a secret list. (Worksheet 1.2, p. 16–18)
_____ Completes list of excuses. (Worksheet 1.3, p.19–21)
_____ Completes consequences inventory. (Worksheet 1.4, p. 23)
_____ Examines ongoing denial using denial worksheet. (Worksheet 1.5, p. 29)
_____ Inventories 14 distortion strategies in personal life. (Worksheet 1.5, p. 30–36)
_____ Makes full disclosure to therapist. (p. 274)

2. Understand the nature of the illness.

_____ Learns definitions of abuse and dependency. (Worksheet 2.1, p. 48)
_____ Understands addictive system. (Figure 2.1, p. 55)
_____ Understands recovery system. (Figure 2.2, p. 63)
_____ Maps out personal addictive system & system transformer. (Figure 2.3, p. 68)
_____ Completes addiction history. (Worksheet 4.1, p. 98)
_____ Understands criteria for addictive illness. (p. 46)
_____ Applies criteria to personal behavior. (p. 48)
_____ Maps brain damage. (Worksheet 3.1, p. 86)
_____ Learns key factors in the genesis of addiction. (p. 46)
_____ Completes complementary addiction worksheet. (Worksheet 7.3, p. 258)

3. Surrenders to process.

_____ Understands existential position on change—essence of recovery. (p. 96)
_____ Completes powerless worksheet. (Worksheet 1.6, p. 38)
_____ Completes unmanageability worksheet. (Worksheet 4.3, p. 108)
_____ Completes financial costs worksheet. (Worksheet 4.4, p. 111)
_____ Identifies ten worst moments. (Worksheet 4.5, p. 116)
_____ Understands guidelines of step completion. (p. 261)
_____ Completes First Step. (Chapter 4)
_____ Completes Higher Power worksheet. (Worksheet 4.6, p. 124)

4. Limits damage from behavior.

_____ Understands first and second order change. (p. 131)
_____ Understands concept of paradigm shift. (p. 134)
_____ Understands provisional beliefs. (p. 134)
_____ Completes damage control plan. (Worksheets 5.3–5.9, p. 139–173)
_____ Completes a disclosure/accountability plan. (Worksheet 5.10, p. 175)

5. Establish sobriety.

_____ Understands sobriety as boundary problem. (p. 183–185)
_____ Understands sobriety challenges. (p. 194)
_____ Completes sobriety challenges worksheet. (Worksheet 6.1, p. 195)
_____ Completes recovery essentials worksheet. (Worksheet 6.2, p. 199)
_____ Understands relapse process. (p. 247–251)
Completes relapse prevention sequence, includes scenario worksheets (Worksheets 6.3–6.5, p. 208–210)
     _____ fire drill planning (Worksheet 6.6, page 212)
     _____ letter to self (p. 243)
     _____ emergency first aid kit (p. 245)
     _____ relapse contract (Worksheet 6.14, p. 246)

_____ Completes Three Circle Boundary Worksheet. (Worksheet 6.10, p. 222)

_____ Begins Use of Personal Craziness Index (PCI). (Worksheet 6.12, p. 233)

_____ Completes personal expectation template. (Worksheet 7.1, p. 255)

6. Ensure physical integrity.

_____ Learns physical aspects of addiction. (Chapter 3)

_____ Detoxes from all chemicals of abuse. (p. 85)

_____ Understands withdrawal/post-acute withdrawal syndrome and impact on the body. (p. 85)

_____ Completes physical. (p. 89)

_____ Completes psychological/psychiatric assessment. (p. 89)

_____ Implement strategies for brain health. (p. 89–92)

7. Participate in a culture of support. (Chapter 8)

_____ Participates in a Twelve Step program.

_____ Develops relationship with sponsor.

_____ Completes sponsor debriefing.

_____ Does service in program.

_____ Knows signs of a healthy group.

_____ Has celebration date.

At this point, you have completed the first seven of the thirty tasks. There are several areas of concern that you ought to think about at this point. First, you need to share what you have done with those who have been part of this process—therapists, sponsors, group mates, and friends. Allow them to congratulate you, and think of some ways that you can thank them for their help. Also, figure out a way to celebrate what you've accomplished. If you are in a Twelve Step program, there may already be a celebration as part of the process. If you are doing this work individually, it is still important to take time to notice what you have accomplished. You deserve much credit for getting this far! At the conclusion of this chapter, we have provided a page on which you can have people write wishes and comments.

Your next challenge is a workbook called *The Recovery Zone*, which takes you from task eight to task nineteen. The remaining tasks are all about family and intimacy and they, too, have their own workbook.

We are grateful that you have taken the risk to live in the solution. All of us share the same challenge our storytellers have discerned as our lot as humans. The stories of Luke Skywalker and Frodo Baggins are not just for entertainment. They are about you and me and making the commitment to change. It matters a great deal that you have made a commitment to change.

Comments and Reflections

You have now completed the tasks of beginning recovery from addiction. What are your reflections, comments, and wishes as you move on to the next challenge? Please take a moment to add your thoughts in celebration of this hard work. Feel free to use a journal or notebook if you need extra space.

_____

_____

_____

_____

For Further Reading

The following list contains books referenced in this book, as well as further readings that you may find helpful.

Beattie, Melody. *Journey to the Heart: Daily Meditations on the Path to Freeing Your Soul.* San Francisco: Harper San Francisco, 1996.

Black, Claudia. *A Hole in the Sidewalk: The Recovering Person's Guide to Relapse Prevention.* Bainbridge, WA: MAC Publishing, 2000.

Bradshaw, John. *Healing the Shame That Binds You.* Deerfield Beach, Fla.: Health Communications, 1988.

Breton, Denise, and Christopher Largent. *The Paradigm Conspiracy: Why Our Social Systems Violate Our Human Potential and How We Can Change Them.* Center City, Minn.: Hazelden, 1996.

Bryan, Mark, and Julia Cameron. *The Money Drunk: Ninety Days to Financial Sobriety.* New York: Ballantine Books, 1993.

Bradshaw, John. *Bradshaw on the Family: A Revolutionary Way of Self-Discovery.* Pompano Beach, Fla.: Health Communications, 1988.

Bradshaw, John. *Family Secrets, What You Don't Know Can Hurt You.* New York: Bantam Books, 1996.

Calof, David L., and Robin Simons. *The Couple Who Became Each Other and Other Tales of Healing of a Master Hypnotherapist.* New York: Bantam Books, 1996.

Cameron, Julia. *The Artist's Way.* New York: Putnam, 1995.

Caring for Yourself. New York: Walker, 1989.

Carnes, Patrick J. *The Betrayal Bond: Breaking Free of Exploitive Relationships.* Deerfield Beach, Fla.: Health Communications, 1998.

Covey, Stephen R. *First Things First: Everyday.* New York: Simon & Schuster, 1999.

Covey, Stephen. *The Seven Habits of Highly Effective People: Powerful Lessons in Personal Change.* New York: Simon & Schuster, 1989.

Eisler, Riane. *The Chalice and the Blade: Our History, Our Future.* San Francisco: Harper & Row, 1987.

Evans, Patricia. *The Verbally Abusive Relationship: How to Recognize It and How to Respond.* Holbrook, Mass.: Adams Media Corporation, 1996.

Fossum, Merle A., and Marilyn J. Mason. *Facing Shame: Families in Recovery.* New York: Norton, 1989.

Friel, John, and Linda Friel. *Adult Children: The Secrets of Dysfunctional Families.* Deerfield Beach, Fla.: Health Communications, 1988.

Hartigan, Francis. *Bill W.: A Biography of Alcoholics Anonymous Cofounder Bill Wilson.* New York: St. Martin's Press, 2000.

Hope and Recovery: The Twelve Step Guide for Healing from Compulsive Sexual Behavior. Center City, Minn.: Hazelden, 1994.

Love, Patricia. *Emotional Incest Syndrome: What to Do When a Parents Love Rules Your Life.* New York: Bantam Books, 1991.

Mellody, Pia, with Andrea Well Miller and J. Keith Miller. *Facing Codependence.* San Francisco: Harper San Francisco, 1989.

Milkman, Harvey B., and Stanley Sunderwirth. *Craving for Ecstasy: The Chemistry and Consciousness of Escape.* New York: Free Press, 1987.

Miller, Alice. *For Your Own Good: Hidden Cruelty in Child-Rearing and the Roots of Violence.* New York: Farrar, Straus, Giroux, 1990.

Millman, Dan. *Way of the Peaceful Warrior: A Book That Changes Lives.* Tiburon, Calif.: Kramer, 1984.

Mueller, Wayne. *Sabbath: Restoring the Sacred Rhythm of Rest.* New York: Bantam, 1999.

Mundis, Jerrold. *How to Get Out of Debt, Stay Out of Debt & Live Prosperously.* New York: Bantam Books, 1990.

Nouwen, Henri J. *The Return of the Prodigal Son: A Story of Homecoming.* New York: Doubleday, 1994.

Nouwen, Henri J. *Reaching Out: The Three Movements of the Spiritual Life.* Garden City, N.Y.: Doubleday, 1986.

Peck, M. Scott. *People of the Lie: The Hope for Healing Human Evil.* New York: Simon & Schuster, 1985.

Peck, M. Scott. *The Road Less Traveled.* New York: Simon & Schuster, 1978.

Robertson, Nan. *Getting Better: Inside Alcoholics Anonymous.* Lincoln, NE: iUniverse.com, 1998, 2000.

Schaeffer, Brenda. *Is It Love or Is It Addiction?, Second Edition.* Center City, Minn: Hazelden, 1997.

Zukav, Gary. *The Seat of the Soul.* New York: Simon & Schuster, 1989. (Especially good chapter on addiction, pp. 148–179)

Resource Guide

The following is a list of recovery fellowships that may be helpful to you in your particular situation.

Adult Children of Alcoholics
310-534-1815
www.adultchildren.org

Alateen (ages 12–17)
800-356-9996
www.al-anon-alateen.org

Al-Anon
800-344-2666
www.al-anon.org

Alcoholics Anonymous
212-870-3400
www.alcoholics-anonymous.org

Co-Dependents Anonymous
602-277-7991
www.codependents.org

Co-Dependents of Sex Addicts
763-537-6904
www.cosa-recovery.org

Cocaine Anonymous
800-347-8998
www.ca.org

CoAnon
520-513-5028
www.co-anon.org

Debtors Anonymous
781-453-2743
www.debtorsanonymous.org

Emotions Anonymous
651-647-9712
www.mtn.org/EA

Families Anonymous
310-815-8010
www.familiesanonymous.org

Gamblers Anonymous
213-386-8789
www.gamblersanonymous.org

**Marijuana
Anonymous**
212-459-4423
www.marijuana-anonymous.org

**Narcotics
Anonymous**
818-773-9999
www.na.org

**Nicotine
Anonymous**
415-750-0328
www.nicotine-anonymous.org

**Overeaters
Anonymous**
505-891-2664
www.oa.org

**Recovering
Couples Anonymous**
781-794-1456
www.recovering-couples.org

**Runaway and
Suicide Hotline**
800-RUN-AWAY
www.1800runaway.org

S-Anon
615-833-3152
www.sanon.org

**Sex and Love Addicts
Anonymous**
www.slaafws.org

**Sex Addicts
Anonymous**
713-869-4902
www.sexaa.org

**Sexaholics
Anonymous**
866-424-8777
www.sa.org

**Sexual Addiction Resources/
Dr. Patrick Carnes**
www.sexhelp.com

**Sexual Compulsives
Anonymous**
310-859-5585
www.sca-recovery.org

**Society for the
Advancement
of Sexual Heath**
706-356-7031
www.sash.net

**Survivors of
Incest Anonymous**
410-282-3400
www.siawso.org